TAUNTON'S

BOOKCASES
BUILT-INS
& CABINETS

The Taunton Press

THE TAUNTON PRESS, INC.
63 South Main Street
Newtown, CT 06470-2344
E-mail: tp@taunton.com

EDITOR: Christina Glennon
INDEXER: Laura Abed
INTERIOR DESIGN: Carol Singer
LAYOUT: Susan Lampe-Wilson

Fine Woodworking® and *Fine Homebuilding*® are trademarks of The Taunton Press, Inc., registered in the U.S. Patent and Trademark Office.

The following names/manufacturers appearing in *Bookcases, Built-Ins & Cabinets* are trademarks: . AplePly®, Comb Light®, DeWalt®, Driller Toggle™, Dual Cut™, Everbilt™, EZ Ancor®, Festool®, FlipToggle®, General Finishes™, Hiddenbed™, Hillman™, iPad®, Lee Valley®, Makita®, Masonite®, Masterforce®, McMaster-Carr®, Medex®, Midwest Fasteners®, Plascore®, Pluma Ply™, Plyboo®, Red Head®, Ridgid®, Rockler®, SealCoat™, Sharpie®, Snaptoggle®, Starrett®, Tapcon®, Titebond®, Toggler®, Toggler Alligator®, TransTint®, Tried & True™, Triple Grip™, X-Acto®.

Library of Congress Control Number: 2022923351

ISBN 978-1-64155-187-8

Printed in the United States of America
10 9 8 7 6 5 4 3 2 1

ABOUT YOUR SAFETY: Working wood is inherently dangerous. Using hand or power tools improperly or ignoring safety practices can lead to permanent injury or even death. Don't try to perform operations you learn about here (or elsewhere) unless you're certain they are safe for you. If something about an operation doesn't feel right, don't do it. Look for another way. We want you to enjoy the craft, so please keep safety foremost in your mind whenever you're in the shop.

DEDICATION

Special thanks to the authors, editors, art directors, copy editors, and other staff members of *Fine Woodworking* and *Fine Homebuilding* who contributed to the development of the chapters in this book.

Contents

PART FOUR

Cabinets

Introduction

There are many elements that make a house feel like a home, including thoughtful storage solutions. Whether it's a smartly designed bookshelf or a hideaway cubby to hold a family's heirloom quilts, smart storage not only organizes your life but also beautifies it at the same time.

Curated from the pages of *Fine Homebuilding* and *Fine Woodworking* magazines, each project in this book was designed and built by one of North America's most talented craftspeople, promising to elevate the feel and function of your home beyond anything you can buy in a store.

In each home I've lived in, I've crafted bookcases, built-ins, and cabinets like the ones in this rich collection. Although I've left behind more than one built-in library, fireplace surround, and kitchen island along the way, I've never regretted the tastefulness and functionality they added to our family life—or the significant resale value they contributed

when we moved. The freestanding pieces, on the other hand, like the bookcases and wall shelves in this book, came with us when we moved or were gifted to friends and family.

While specific dimensions are given for each project, all are meant to be sized and adapted to your own personal taste, space, and needs. That's the beauty of custom work. What's more, the artisans who produced them are experienced makers with very reliable techniques. So whether you build the specific project pictured or use a similar approach to build something totally different, you'll be gaining fundamental skills and knowledge you can put to work for many years to come.

I invite you dig into this collection, find a project that inspires you, and start making your home your own.

—*Asa Christiana is the former editor of* Fine Woodworking *magazine and the author of the "Build Stuff with Wood" book series.*

Guide to Sheet Goods

SUZANNE WALTON AND
OWEN MADDEN

Rowan Woodwork is a small team of design-and-build nerds nestled in the former New York State capital of Kingston. Much of what we do is cabinetry, such as kitchens, bathrooms and vanities, wardrobes, offices, and libraries. We specialize in modern European cabinets, which have opened our scope to many different types of plywood and other sheet goods.

The choices on the market are endless and constantly evolving and changing. But the ones we present here are our current go-to sheet goods for cabinetry work. With these 11 products we can pull off any look—from Shaker-inspired to sleek, minimalist, and modern—and any finish, from painted to natural to oiled and waxed. Every project is different, and availability isn't always consistent; knowing each product's strengths and weaknesses allows us to have options and tailor the materials to the specific project, with the goal being a gorgeous end result that will stand the test of time and use.

Where MDF excels. These large doors and drawers showcase MDF's strengths. It offers a flat, void-free, stable surface to hold the sequenced walnut veneers.

MDF: Flat, smooth, and stable

Because it's an engineered material, MDF doesn't have grain patterns, which gives it a smooth finish ideal for paint or veneer, and a consistent, stable thickness. An MDF core panel with a pre-applied veneer is the absolute best product for cabinet doors and drawers. Completely void-free, it makes for a very flat surface, and the fibrous core won't move while it's being cut or after installation.

NAMES: MDF, MDF Core (veneered)

USES: Best for cabinet doors/drawers. Painted surfaces. Nonstructural veneered surfaces.

PRICE*: MDF $65 for a ¼-in. by 4-ft. by 8-ft. sheet MDF Core (veneered) $100-$150 (depending on species of veneer) for a ¾-in. by 4-ft. by 8-ft. sheet

AVAILABILITY: Most specialty plywood dealers and some home centers.

SIZES: Sheets come in widths of 4 ft. and 5 ft. with lengths up to 10 ft. and thickness ranging from ¼ in. to 1 in.

COLORS: Available in a variety of veneers.

PROS: Flat and very stable, easily veneered with any material, low cost.

CONS: Less structural than veneer core, susceptible to moisture. Formaldehyde-based products are known to be harmful. Heavy.

Out-of-the-box MDF use. The client specifically wanted an MDF core with a linear rift white oak veneer for an ultramodern look. Typically, Rowan's designers prefer not to make the structural portions of millwork out of MDF, but the design incorporated lots of vertical support and small spans, so the MDF worked fine. It provided a flat, stable surface and gave the client the look they wanted.

Medex: A better MDF

Think of Medex as MDF's hippie younger brother. This product has all the great qualities of basic MDF and a few more. Made with recycled wood and no added formaldehyde resin, it is very environmentally friendly. With a list a mile long of its environmental achievements, it also manages to be more water-resistant than other fiberboards.

NAMES: Medex, Medex MDF, SDF (sustainable design fiberboard)

USES: Best for painted cabinet faces, trim, or panels. It can be veneered with any material and makes a great, stable substrate.

PRICE*: $90 for a ¾-in. by 4-ft. by 8-ft. sheet

AVAILABILITY: Widely available at specialty plywood dealers.

SIZES: Sheets come 4 ft. and 5 ft. wide, with lengths up to 18 ft. and thickness ranging from ¼ in. to 1¼ in.

COLORS: Natural (brown), black, and gray

PROS: Consistent thickness, not much movement based on moisture, paints very well, no core so no need to edge-band if painting.

CONS: Less structural than veneer core, easily damaged, creates lots of very fine dust.

Perfect for paint. In this Shaker-style kitchen, Rowan used solid poplar for the rails and stiles and Medex for the panels. It is not only a more environmentally friendly material than MDF, but it also finishes better.

*Pricing on sheet goods can vary widely by distributor and can change daily.

Veneer-core plywood

Veneer-core plywood is an extremely useful material because it is easily available, very sturdy, structural, and extremely stable if made well. When clients want wood faces for casework, opt for the strength and screw-holding power of plywood for the boxes. You also can use 1-in. veneer core for shelves as it is stronger than MDF, which tends to sag.

NAMES: Veneer core (unfinished), Veneer-core plywood C2 MPBY (Columbia forest products)

USES: Unfinished veneer-core plywood excels in situations where structural integrity is necessary and aesthetics such as wood species and finish need to be tailored to the job.

PRICE*: $80 for a ¾-in. by 4-ft. by 8-ft. sheet

AVAILABILITY: Most specialty plywood dealers and some home centers.

SIZES: Sheets come in 4-ft. widths and lengths up to 10 ft., with thickness from ½ in. to 1 in.

COLORS: Various options based on veneer, distributor, and manufacturer. Columbia Forest Products offers a large selection of hardwood face veneers, such as maple, alder, hickory, cherry, walnut, oak, and sapele to name a few.

PROS: Structural, choice of wood species for veneer, apply finish of choice, inexpensive.

CONS: Voids and telegraphing of imperfections in core, visible core requires edge-banding or a face frame.

Sequenced and matched. Rowan applied this walnut veneer to veneer-core plywood. They specifically used veneer core for its ability to hold a screw. In a kitchen where the fridge has an integrated panel and mounting brackets, veneer core's superior screw holding makes it a much better choice than MDF for the panel.

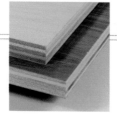

Prefinished plywood

Prefinished maple plywood is the ultimate cabinetmaker's workhorse. With a tough satin finish already applied, it makes for quick construction of the basic casework. We use a Maple C2 grade traditional veneer core; it is a mid-grade face, but to alter our favorite Bob Van Dyke quote, "the plates won't mind," the clothes inside won't either. Some manufacturers, like Columbia Forest, with Pure-Bond, use a soy-based and non-formaldehyde formula glue and finish in their plywood. This makes their prefinished plywood environmentally friendly, which is always a plus.

NAME: Prefinished plywood

USES: Best for cabinet interiors. It's available with finish on one face or both, so it can work for sides, backs, and shelving.

PRICE*: $95 for a ¾-in. by 4-ft. by 8-ft. sheet

AVAILABILITY: Most specialty plywood dealers and some home centers.

SIZES: Sheets come in widths of 4 ft. and lengths up to 10 ft. with thickness ranging from ½ in. to 1 in.

COLORS: Options for color are based on veneer: maple, walnut, oak, cherry, and sapele.

PROS: Not having to finish cabinet interiors is always a huge pro! Structural, inexpensive.

CONS: Only one finish is available. Voids and telegraphing of imperfections in the core.

Perfect for cabinet interiors. Rowan uses prefinished maple for most of their cabinet interiors. The tough, pre-applied satin finish works perfectly for anything you want to throw inside it. Additionally, the maple has warm neutral tones that won't distract from whatever material you use for the cabinet faces.

*Pricing on sheet goods can vary widely by distributor and can change daily.

Baltic birch

The gold standard of multi-ply plywood, and the most widely available product, Baltic birch is more dense and rigid than classic cores or any other basic hardwood plywood. Its uses range from sturdy cabinets to shop jigs to fine furniture. Baltic birch is plywood made of an odd number of layers of birch hardwood (usually imported from the Baltic Sea region) crossbanded and sanded flat, making for a dense, void-free core with more layers than a typical sheet. There are different options in glue, allowing uses that range from indoor cabinetry to outdoor and light marine uses.

NAMES: Baltic birch, Russian birch

USES: Painted cabinet faces, trim, or panels. It can be veneered with any material and makes a great stable substrate.

PRICE*: $130 for a ¾-in. by 4-ft. by 8-ft. sheet

AVAILABILITY: Lumberyard or home center, also online from websites like Rockler, Woodcraft, and even Amazon.

SIZES: Sheets come in widths of 4 ft., 5 ft., or 8 ft., lengths up to 8 ft., and thickness ranging from ⅛ in. to 1 in.

COLORS: No options for color. Birch veneer top sheets.

PROS: More sturdy than classic veneer-core plywood, indoor and outdoor use, lots of size and thickness options, clear hardwood face typical of B1 grade. Excellent screw-holding power. Edges can be exposed without edge-banding for a modern/industrial/European look.

CONS: More expensive than veneer-core, fewer options for face grain.

The go-to utility ply. Used here as drawer dividers inside a solid-wood drawer box, Baltic birch gives a higher-end look to something that can tend to be mundane.

ApplePly

When you're after that exposed edge look, ApplePly is another great option. Like its European multi-ply competition, it has a lot more ply layers than typical plywood (both have 13 plies per ¾ in.), making for a very good aesthetic. ApplePly is manufactured in the United States using a mix of aspen and maple trees, setting it apart from the birch and poplar hardwood cores used in Baltic birch and Russian birch. ApplePly is available with a variety of hardwood face veneers and measures up to the best quality European competitors.

NAME: ApplePly

USES: Sturdy cabinetry, exposed-edge furniture and cabinetry, outdoor or high moisture–exposed millwork.

PRICE*: $180 for a ¾-in. by 4-ft. by 8-ft. sheet

AVAILABILITY: Some specialty plywood dealers and online at buyappleply.com

SIZES: Sheets come in widths of 4 ft., lengths up to 8 ft., with thickness ranging from ¼ in. to 1½ in.

COLORS: Based on veneer options; maple, walnut, oak, cherry, birch, and teak.

PROS: Able to finish the edge without edge-banding, more sturdy than classic veneer-core plywood, indoor and outdoor use, lots of size and thickness options, made in America. It has almost no voids, is very flat, strong, and consistent in thickness. Excellent screw-holding power.

CONS: Expensive, limited veneer options.

As American as ApplePly. This domestic multi-ply is a fantastic alternative to Baltic birch or other European birch plywood. Here it's used specifically for its unique exposed edge, but also leaning on its stronger core to bear the weight in this modern desk and shelving.

Multi-ply with a tough finish

The top-of-the-line multi-ply with the widest array of uses, this material is super stable and very durable. It is a Swiss army knife (or perhaps a Finnish army knife) in a world of plastic utensils. FinPly is very similar to Baltic-birch plywood but with a phenolic resin coating, which makes this a durable prefinished alternative to original Baltic birch. One of the most versatile materials on the market, its uses range from concrete forms to high-end cabinetry and millwork.

NAMES: FinPly, Phenolic plywood, Colorfin Ply, Euro Color Ply

USES: Exposed-edge furniture and millwork, exterior paneling, shop tabletops, and jigs.

PRICE*: $290 for a ¾-in. by 4-ft. by 8-ft. sheet.

AVAILABILITY: Some specialty plywood dealers such as Roberts Plywood. Woodcraft and Amazon in smaller sizes.

SIZES: Sheets up to 4 ft. by 8 ft. with thickness ranging from ½ in. to ¾ in.

COLORS: White, yellow, orange, red, green, blue, gray, black, and natural clear.

PROS: Stability, durability, void-free core for exposed-edge furniture or cabinetry, beautiful colors and finish, resistant to moisture.

CONS: Very expensive, difficult to find, touching up the phenolic finish is near impossible. The phenolic coating can chip while cutting.

European modern design. Rowan used FinPly, a phenolic resin-coated birch veneer multi-ply, for all the casework in this bar and shelving unit, creating a sanded, chamfered, oiled, and waxed edge to achieve the aesthetic that the clients requested.

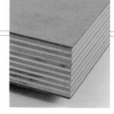

Plywood meets fiberboard

Garnica or Pluma Ply is a hybrid sheet good with an ultralight poplar ply core and HDF (high density fiberboard) face material on top that can be veneered, laminated, or painted. It has become one of the most coveted products on the shelf in our shop. We use it for anything from simple shop jigs and fixtures to the structural panels holding together our most intricate cabinetry. It is a lightweight, void-free alternative to regular ply and a more structural choice than MDF.

NAMES: Garnica, Pluma Ply

USES: Best for painted cabinet casework, lightweight structural panels, shop fixtures.

PRICE*: $110 for a ¾-in. by 4-ft. by 8-ft. sheet

AVAILABILITY: Most specialty plywood dealers

SIZES: Sheets come in widths of 4 ft. and 5 ft., lengths up to 10 ft., with thickness ranging from ½ in. to 2 in.

COLORS: Brown is the only option.

PROS: Easy to paint, holds a screw better than classic MDF/HDF, void and knot-free, little movement. Lightweight.

CONS: A bit more expensive, visible core needs edge-banding or face frame.

Your framing friend. Garnica is an ideal material for framing. It is flat, strong, light, and easier to rip into dimensional parts than wonky 2x material. Rowan frequently uses it in places such as inside a kitchen island, creating a chase for the electrical and plumbing. Or here, as the infrastructure holding a built-in bed together.

*Pricing on sheet goods can vary widely by distributor and can change daily.

Eco-friendly bamboo

For the environmentally minded, bamboo has been a shining star in the sustainable building industry. Plyboo has a selection of stunning and eco-friendly sheet products with different cores and layups to match any project you have in mind. Plyboo is made of either three or four layers of fast-growing bamboo. Instead of a roll cut of veneer between the layers, these strips are glued up more like a classic solid-wood lamination, making the sheets very stable, architecturally rated, and 100% rapidly renewable. As a sheet good, the classic look of the ancient material takes on a modern aesthetic.

NAMES: Plyboo, Plyboo plywood (Smith and Fong)

USES: Indoor cabinetry faces, interiors, or wall paneling.

PRICE*: $220 for a ¾-in. by 4-ft. by 8-ft. sheet

AVAILABILITY: Some specialty plywood dealers such as Eco Supply

SIZES: Sheets come in 4 ft. by 8 ft. with thickness ranging from ¼ in. to 1 in.

COLORS: Natural and amber.

PROS: 100% rapidly renewable, stable core.

CONS: Expensive, extremely hard (dulls blades and bits), chips easily when cut.

Sleek and sustainable. Plyboo is a fantastic product that is a green alternative to regular ply veneer. It is sustainably made and can do any job other materials can do but with less of a carbon footprint, which can be very important to some clients.

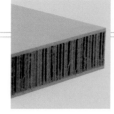

Honeycomb core for light weight

Think of these products as a futuristic model for what plywoods might become. The core of this sci-fi sheet good is made of materials including fiber, cardboard, foam, and PC2 polycarbonate plastic. This substrate will keep any panel rigid, flat, and super-light. The product's core, in a grid resembling a bees' honeycomb, is sandwiched between thin skins of HDF or MDF; the combination creates a strong, lightweight torsion box that won't twist or bow.

NAMES: Plascore PC2, Polycarbonate Honeycomb, Comb Light

USES: Best as a thick, light substrate, such as in a thick wall panel detail or oversized door.

PRICE*: $90 for a ½-in. by 4-ft. by 8-ft. sheet

AVAILABILITY: Plascor.com, Thinklightweight.com

SIZES: Sheets up to 60 in. by 150 in. with thickness ranging from ⅛ in. to 2 in.

COLORS: Black, white, or clear depending on dealer.

PROS: Stable, very light, avoids twisting, unaffected by moisture.

CONS: Hard to find, not very versatile.

Fun use of Plascore. For these 30-in. by 8-ft. doors, the designers used a poplar frame with a polypropylene honeycomb core and an MDF veneer. The result is an ultralight and stable door that moves easily, finishes well, and stays dead flat over the years.

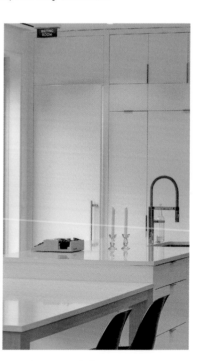

All You Need Is a Track Saw

JUSTIN FINK

When I got my first track saw years ago, it was an absolute game changer for my trim carpentry work. No more trying to shove full sheets of plywood through a small job-site tablesaw. But for those first few years, I was really only using the track saw to break down sheets of plywood into their rough parts, which I would then run through the tablesaw for final sizing. I didn't have confidence in my ability to get consistently sized parts, say for building a bank of cabinets, without the aid of a fence. But as I've refined my techniques, I now feel comfortable processing a stack of plywood into a variety of consistently sized parts and pieces, all without a tablesaw.

Track-saw setups are available from Festool, Makita, and DeWalt, among others. But keep in mind that many parts of these systems are cross-compatible. My saw and tracks are both made by Festool, but the zero-clearance strip on the track, and the clamps I use to secure it to sheet goods, are both made by DeWalt. Similarly, my dust hose is made by Bosch, and I often connect it to a Ridgid vac.

Whichever tools you use, accurate cuts require a thoughtful sequence. I've tried lots of different workflows for processing sheet

Get set up

Clean-edged, accurate track-saw cuts require a well-tuned saw, sawblade, and track. Here's my prework checklist for clean, accurate cuts.

THE SAW AND TRACK

- The saw should engage snugly with the grooves in the track, and the blade should align perfectly with the outer edge of the zero-clearance strip on the track. If it doesn't, readjust the saw on the track and take a fresh cut to zero out the strip.
- Make sure the zero-clearance strip is adhered to the track completely. If the adhesive has started to let go, buy and install a replacement.
- The saw should always be hooked to a vac. Most importantly, it's healthy. But it also keeps sawdust from interfering with layout and solid contact between the track and sheet, and extends the life of the sawblade.

THE WORK SITE

- Ample light, ideally slightly raking, is crucial for layout. If possible, locate the work so the light source is on the cutting side of the track rather than straight above or behind it. Even a small shadow cast by the zero-clearance strip can lead to misaligned cuts.
- To fully support the workpiece in every direction, make all cuts atop a sacrificial 4x8 sheet of rigid foam set on a stable worktable, not spanning sawhorses. If storing the foam is an issue, cut the sheet into thirds, then tape the pieces back together to create a fanfold arrangement.
- When it comes to accurate layout and cuts, don't underestimate the value of a tape measure that's in good condition, and a super-sharp pencil. For the latter, use a high-quality pencil with a fairly hard lead of at least H or 2H, and keep it sharp.

Good light

You should be able to clearly see the pencil line.

Bad light

Shadows make it hard to see the pencil line.

goods—laying out the full sheet while trying to account for sawkerfs, cutting each piece out one at a time, and more. I find the method shown here to be the most efficient, and it's become my standard practice. After establishing two edges that are square to each other, work from one side of the sheet to the other. Group parts by their width, which allows you to focus first on the long rip cuts. Then those rip cuts can be crosscut to their final length, either individually or as a group.

Always start square

Never, ever trust the factory edges on a piece of plywood. You can't assume they're straight, or square to each other.

Create a clean edge. If you want quality results, the first cut should always be along the length of the plywood, about ¼ in. to ½ in. in from the edge. I set the track for this first rip cut by eye, because at this point the goal is simply to get a straight cut, not be dead parallel or square.

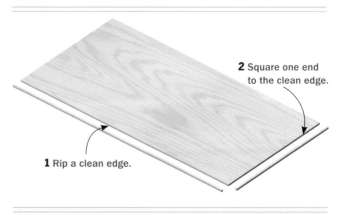

2 Square one end to the clean edge.

1 Rip a clean edge.

Clamp or no clamp? Track-saw tracks have grippy strips to help them stay in place, so technically you don't need clamps unless you're cutting melamine, prefinished plywood, or a sheet with some other slick surface. Still, a pair of clamps can cost less than a single sheet of plywood, and will ensure you start right on the cut marks and stay that way, even if the cord or hose catches the track.

Square up the end of the sheet. Use the one long, clean edge as a reference to create a second clean, square edge. A framing square is too small for this work. Either square up using measurements and a 3/4/5 triangle, or get a big folding layout square (available from C.H. Hanson). Again, keep the cut close to the factory end of the sheet to maximize the stock.

Rip cuts first

With two fresh-cut, square edges to work from, move on to the long rip cuts. Each cut is laid out with two measurements, one at each end of the sheet.

Measure accurately. Hold the tape parallel to the edge you're measuring, and roll it down flat to the surface with two fingers while marking between.

Drop the track. After marking both ends of the sheet, position the track on the sheet so that the zero-clearance strip is aligned with the pencil marks on both ends.

Double-check. With the clamp in the track but left loose, measure again—this time from the cutting edge of the track back to the clean edge of the plywood—confirming you're still dead on layout before clamping the track in position.

Smooth cutting. Let the blade get up to full speed before plunging to your preset depth and advancing into the edge of the plywood. With the track secured, one hand pushes the saw and the other guides the hose and power cord to avoid snags.

Trick for narrow rips. When ripping pieces narrower than the width of the track, use double-stick carpet tape to hold the piece down to the foam, and an offcut of the same thickness to help support the track.

Then crosscuts

There are a few options for making crosscuts. The method you choose depends on the width of the piece to be cut and the number of same-size pieces you need to create.

The basic cut. As long as the piece to be crosscut isn't more than about 24 in. wide, the fastest method is to measure along one edge of the piece, mark the length, and use a framing square to mark the cutline. If it's wider than 24 in., revert to the method for marking rip cuts.

Check Your Square For Square

Framing squares are sometimes out-of-square right from the factory; other times they get dropped or otherwise damaged. The best way to check is to hold the square against a clean, straight-edged piece of plywood and strike a pencil line along the square's blade. Then flip the square over, strike a second line, and see if the two lines are parallel. If they aren't, it's time for a new square.

Cutting narrow pieces. Often pieces will be too narrow for easy clamping, and the overhanging length of the track becomes a hassle. Unless you have a short track for these cuts, put offcuts under the overhanging end of the track so you can use the clamps.

Gang cuts. Many jobs involve multiple sheets with multiple pieces of the same size. In these cases, align the pieces, clamp them together, and cut them as a group.

Quick chops. If the pieces to be crosscut are narrow enough to handle with a miter saw, that's a better option. It's fast, and—if you need many parts cut to the same length—allows you the option to use a stop block.

Lightweight Crosscut Sled for Big Panels

STEVE FIKAR

I cut out large plywood parts pretty regularly for a variety of woodworking projects, including cabinets for the house and shop. Ripping these big pieces on the tablesaw is easy enough, but crosscutting them accurately is a challenge. A tablesaw crosscut sled will do the trick, of course, but if you stick to the usual design, a large-capacity sled tends to be very heavy. So I decided to start with a clean slate and engineer something unique.

My solution is an extralarge sled that runs along one side of the blade—instead of straddling it—guided by a single runner in one of the miter slots. To add size and capacity to the sled without adding weight, I borrowed a common engineering solution—torsion-box construction—to create a ⅜-in.-thick base that is very lightweight yet remarkably stiff and strong.

As they are on all crosscut sleds, the fence and base on this sled are trimmed by the blade, creating zero-clearance support for chip-free cuts and easier alignment. An advantage of a one-sided sled is that only one fence is needed, attached at the front edge.

Torsion box base is the key. Fikar used three layers of ⅛-in.-thick tempered hardboard—two full outer layers with a grid of strips between—to create a large base that is both stiff and lightweight. The resulting three-layer sandwich is much lighter and more rigid than a comparable sheet of plywood.

Base Is a Light, Strong Honeycomb

This three-layer sandwich is glued up all at once, so be sure you have everything on hand before starting.

#8–32 machine screws

Top and bottom layers, tempered hardboard, ⅛ in. thick by 30½ in. by 36½ in. after assembly

Strips, tempered hardboard, ⅛ in. thick by 1 in. wide

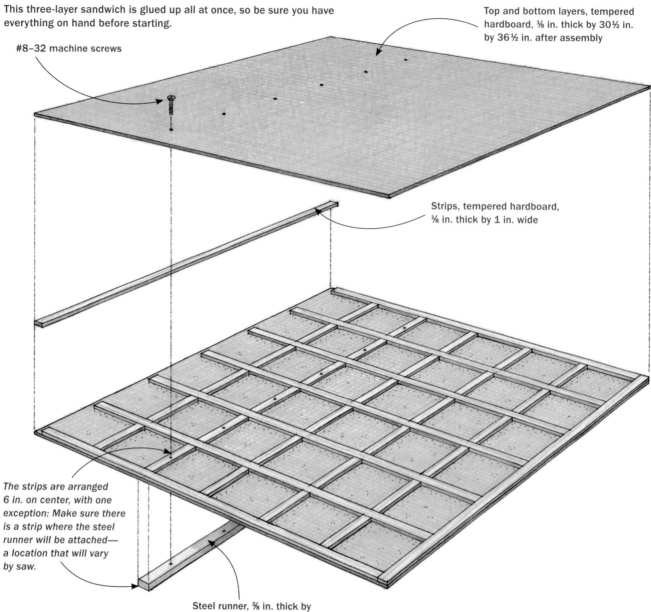

The strips are arranged 6 in. on center, with one exception: Make sure there is a strip where the steel runner will be attached— a location that will vary by saw.

Steel runner, ⅜ in. thick by ¾ in. wide by 36 in. long, tapped for #8–32 machine screws

Gluing up the base. Start by clamping two long strips along adjacent edges, and build out the grid, applying a bead of glue on each piece. Run a bead along the top of the strips and drop the top in place. If you don't have a vacuum bag, you can clamp this big glue-up by laying a piece of plywood on top to distribute pressure, and then piling on every heavy object you own, spread out as evenly as possible.

Attach the steel runner. To resist wear and ensure accuracy for years to come, Fikar uses a steel bar to guide his one-sided sled. To drill and tap it for machine screws, start with a smaller drill bit before stepping up to the full-size #29 (or %₆₄-in.) bit. Lubricate a #8-32 tap and twist it slowly until it starts to cut, trying to keep it square to the bar as you go. Twist until you encounter stiff resistance, then reverse the tap to break off the chips and continue. Then test the threads with a screw. If it's too tight to turn by hand, run the tap through once more. Then deburr the holes with a countersink or deburring bit.

Steel runner ensures accuracy

The main disadvantage of a one-sided sled, especially a large one with heavy cargo, is the single runner that guides it. If it were made from wood, it would tend to wear and get sloppy over time. So I used a steel bar for this sled—"cold-rolled" at the factory to precise dimensions—which will deliver a lifetime of accurate cuts.

Most tablesaw miter-gauge slots are milled to fit a straight bar exactly ¾ in. wide by ⅜ in. thick. You can buy a steel bar with these precise dimensions from a variety of online retailers, in a 3-ft. length that's perfect for this project.

Just to be sure, though, measure your miter slots with a dial caliper and read the specs

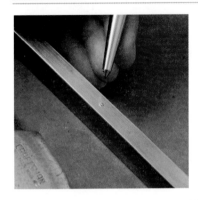

TIP Adjusting the fit of the bar. If the steel bar is loose in the miter slot, improve the fit by dimpling the sides at regular intervals, using a center punch, then filing the dimples as needed. You can check to see which dimples are rubbing by putting ink on them before trying the fit.

carefully on the bar you're considering. The one I found at McMaster-Carr is perfect for my saw, with a tolerance range from a few thousandths undersize up to 0.750 in. on the nose. If there's any doubt, err toward a slightly undersize bar and dimple it to fit, as shown above.

Screw the bar in place. After clamping the bar to the base, drill through each tapped hole with a bit that just clears the threads, then remove the bar and enlarge the holes with a ⁵⁄₃₂-in. bit. Flip the base over and countersink the holes on the top side. The #8-32 machine screws pull the bar tightly to the base. If they stick out past the bottom of the bar, grind or file them flush.

Offcuts are supported too—The other disadvantage of a one-sided sled is the lack of support for cutoff workpieces. Whenever this might be an issue, I place a simple ⅜-in.-thick support piece on the right side of the saw table.

Start by building the torsion-box base

The top and bottom layers of the base are full sheets of hardboard, while the middle layer is a grid of 1-in.-wide strips with open spaces between, making the base somewhat hollow yet extremely stiff.

To get ready for the glue-up, cut the top and bottom pieces slightly oversize, and cut up all of the strips, both the full-length and 5-in.-long ones. Now lay out the grid on the lower layer.

The grid is 6 in. on center with one exception: You need to make sure there is a hardboard strip where the steel runner will be mounted, based on your particular saw design. To keep track of the bar location, I place a strip of blue tape under that area, which I wrap over the edge of the glue-up later. When locating the bar, make sure the right side of the base will bypass the blade by at least ⅛ in., so the blade will trim that edge.

Squaring the fence. To square the fence, create a pivot point by driving a screw through the base and into the fence at the right end. Then simply clamp the left end while you make test cuts and dial in the fence position. Start by trimming the base. Drop the runner into the miter slot and cut the edge of the sled flush to the blade. Then use a circular saw and guide fence to trim the front edge square. The other edges can be ripped parallel on the tablesaw.

The glue-up is straightforward but you have to do it all at once. So make sure you have everything ready to go beforehand, including the plywood and weights for the top layer, and a full bottle of Titebond III (allows 15 minutes of working time).

Find or create a firm, flat surface large enough to support the pieces, and start by gluing the gridwork of strips to the bottom layer. A wide bead of glue on each strip is all it takes.

To keep the pieces from sliding around as you press them into place, start by clamping

Test cuts ensure squareness. Drive a screw through the base into the right end of the fence and clamp the left end. Using a large piece of plywood with its two long edges ripped parallel, make a test cut (above left). Then flip the piece so the opposite long edge is against the sled's fence and feel along the blade side of the base to see if the sled and test cut still align (above right). If they don't, adjust the clamped end of the fence and make another cut. Once the fence is square, drive the full row of screws (right).

two full-length strips along two adjacent edges. Then push the others against those as you build out the grid from there. None of the rest require clamping.

Once the strips are all down and aligned, lay another bead of glue along their top edges and wait a few minutes to let the lower glue-lines stiffen a bit. Now lay down the top sheet of hardboard carefully, making sure that all the strips stay flat with no overlaps. Lay a piece of plywood on top as a clamping caul, and then add as much weight as you can, keeping it even and well distributed.

Fit and attach the bar and fence

The only good way to attach the steel runner to such a thin base is with machine screws that pass through the base and thread into the bar. So you'll need to drill eight evenly spaced holes down the center of the bar and cut #8-32 threads in them. See the photos on p. 19 for how to tap and fit the bar.

Before attaching the bar, check that it's at least ½ in. shorter than the front-to-back length of the sled. That's important because you'll cut the base to final size only after the bar has been attached. Once the bar is screwed on you'll trim the edge of the base that passes the blade; then you'll use a circular saw and a fence to trim the front edge square. You can rip the other edges parallel on the tablesaw.

Attaching the fence perfectly 90° to the path of the blade is easy if you follow the directions in the photos on the facing page. I applied a clear oil finish to my sled for looks and durability, and I wax the bottom and the runner periodically.

Get the most from your new sled

Since the sled starts well in front of the saw table for large workpieces, I add a special

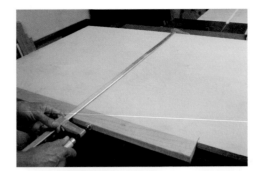

Align and clamp. After the tablesaw blade cuts through the fence, it becomes a zero-clearance indicator for lining up cuts. To make sure large workpieces don't shift, Fikar clamps them to the fence.

Keep the sled from tipping. This long, straight board clamps to the left, front edge of the saw table, supporting the sled and keeping it level when it overhangs the front edge of the saw.

Support large offcuts. Fikar uses this simple jig—equal to the thickness of the sled base—to keep offcuts from dropping off the sled and chipping.

support board to my saw, to help keep the sled level. It clamps to the left edge of the table, extending back several feet toward the user.

To maintain the zero-clearance base and fence, I always use the same blade with this sled. But if the edge ever needs refreshing, you can cut it back a little, add a solid-wood strip, plane it flush on the top and bottom, and re-cut the edge. The fence can also be renewed or replaced if necessary.

Anchor Your Work to the Wall

MARIO RODRIGUEZ

You've finished building your cabinet, mirror, picture frame, or shelf. Now you just need to hang it. If you can hit studs with every screw, you're in good shape. But if not, you'll need wall anchors, those little devices you set into the wall to receive screws or bolts. There's a plethora of anchors out there. Which type is best in your case? That will depend on the size and weight of the piece you're hanging and the composition of the wall you're hanging it on. I've gathered a wide range of anchors, and I'll describe how they work, what situations and wall types they're suited for, and how to install them.

One note before you get to the point of selecting anchors: Be sure to build in some means to easily install or hang your piece. For a cabinet that will carry a lot of weight or see heavy use, you might consider using a thicker back panel, or you could incorporate an inset top rail to keep the piece square and to better support your fasteners. Using a French cleat (see the photo below) adds some time to your build but provides solid attachment, makes the cabinet easily removable, and keeps you from having to drive screws through the cabinet from inside. If you're hanging a stock cabinet (obtained from a box store or cabinet wholesaler), inspect its construction and, if need be, add any cleats, rails, or corner blocks that will strengthen the piece and ensure an easier installation.

Sometimes just a screw will do

For some light-duty applications, like smaller picture frames or a light display shelf, you can actually use coarse-threaded screws designed to be driven into drywall without an anchor or a pilot hole. They're rated to hold as much weight as plastic sleeve anchors, and they have the advantage of leaving a relatively small hole when you extract them. Lee Valley sells Wall Dog Screws (1), which have very nice bite in drywall and are rated at 60 lb.; they can also be used in masonry (or wood) if you drill a pilot hole. Bear Claw Screws (2), also available from Lee Valley, have a flange below the head, making them well-suited for frames or light mirrors that you are hanging with picture wire. They're rated at 30 lb. in drywall.

Self-drilling anchors

You drive these clever anchors into drywall with a screwdriver, no predrilling required. I like their speed and ease of use. Their coarse threads really bite into the wallboard, but they are easily removed and leave little damage. Some have a solid shank so that after a screw is driven into them they simply expand somewhat; others are scored along the shank so the tip splits open behind the drywall for greater holding power.

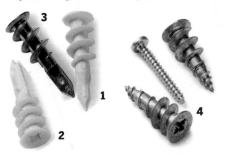

The EZ Ancor Drywall Anchor (1), rated for 50 lb., has a solid shank that expands as the screw is driven; Toggler Self-Drilling Drywall Anchors (2), rated for 65 lb., scissor open when the screw is driven; EZ Ancor zinc drywall anchors (3), rated for 50 lb., can self-drill even if you happen to hit wood behind the drywall; EZ Ancor Drywall and Stud Anchors (4), rated for 50 lb., have a coarsely threaded shank for drywall and a finely threaded tip that enables it to grip a stud behind the drywall.

Expanding anchors

PLASTIC SLEEVE ANCHORS

These anchors are suitable for light-duty tasks like hanging pictures, curtain rods, small shelves, towel rods, and paper holders. You predrill for them, and they work in plaster-and-lath walls and

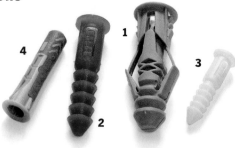

masonry as well as in drywall. Some merely expand when the screw is driven in; others, like the Cobra Triple Grip, have wings that will flip out behind the drywall. Some of the smaller ones require only a small predrilled hole and therefore very little repair when they're removed. Removing the ones with wings can be a chore, and sometimes I just drive them farther into the wall and spackle over the hole.

The Cobra Triple Grip (1), intended for all wall types, is rated for 46–61 lb. in drywall, 200–225 lb. in masonry; Everbilt Ribbed Plastic Anchors (2 and 3), which come in kits of assorted sizes, are rated for 20–25 lb. in drywall, 155–435 lb. in concrete; Duo Power plastic anchors (4) elbow open and are rated for 45 lb.

BUTTERFLY ANCHORS

Butterfly anchors have wings that spread open behind a sheetrock wall. They come in different sizes to suit drywall of various thicknesses. The standard type, like the Hillman Pop Toggle (1), rated for 80 lb., is only suitable with drywall. It requires a large predrilled hole and won't hold well if the wings don't deploy behind the wall. But the Toggler Alligator Concrete and Drywall Anchor (2), while it has wings that will open behind drywall, has a slimmer shank that will expand or scissor open in a predrilled hole, making it suitable for use in masonry walls as well. They are rated for 70 lb. in drywall and 675 lb. in concrete.

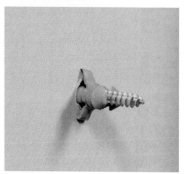
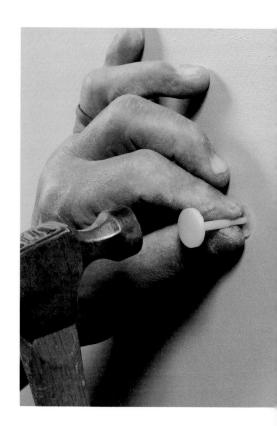

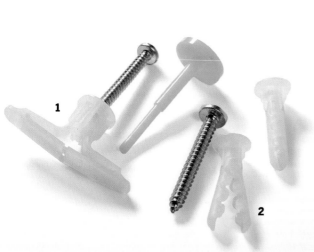

Squeeze the wings and hammer the anchor home. After predrilling, fold the anchor's wings together and push it into the hole, then tap it home with a hammer until the flange is flush with the wall surface. With the anchor in place, use the supplied plastic pusher to pop open the wings (photo facing page). Then drive the screw.

Molly bolts

Molly bolts have a slotted sleeve that will spread open behind a hollow wall when you tighten the machine-threaded screw, creating powerful purchase. They work best with drywall but can also be used in a plaster-and-lath wall. After you predrill and insert the anchor, tapping the sleeve's flange tight to the wall, you begin driving the screw. Small spurs beneath the flange prevent the anchor from spinning in the hole before the sleeve expands. These Midwest Hollow Wall Anchors are rated for 100 lb.

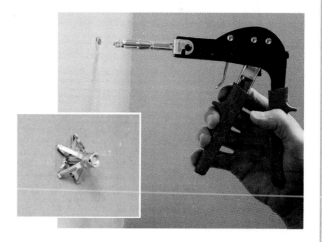

Setting tool for molly bolts. The old-style molly has a newfangled partner. Slip the bolt into the gun's tip and the anchor into the clearance hole. Pull the trigger and the anchor's legs expand, locking it tight. Very handy for setting a lot of mollys.

Toggle anchors

TOGGLE BOLTS

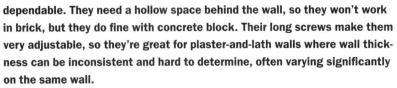

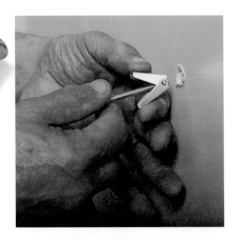

When I need to secure larger cabinets or other wooden pieces to a drywall or plaster wall and there is no stud accessible, toggle bolts are the anchors I most often turn to. Composed of a bolt and a threaded, spring-loaded toggle, they're simple and dependable. They need a hollow space behind the wall, so they won't work in brick, but they do fine with concrete block. Their long screws make them very adjustable, so they're great for plaster-and-lath walls where wall thickness can be inconsistent and hard to determine, often varying significantly on the same wall.

After you've drilled through the wall, the inserted toggle must clear the wall material far enough to spring open; they won't work otherwise, so make sure to use a long enough screw to get the toggle clear of the wall. Properly installed, these anchors have a very positive feel. Once the screws are tightened, there is little doubt that the cabinet they are holding is secure and strong. The Everbilt toggle bolt above is rated for 95 lb. in drywall, 90 lb. in hollow block.

SELF-DRILLING TOGGLE

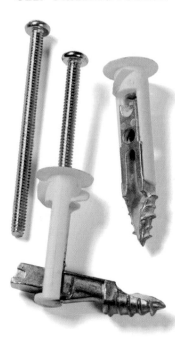

The Cobra Driller Toggle is a very clever hybrid anchor, marrying self-drilling capability with toggle action. The metal toggle, which is hinged to a split plastic shaft, is threaded at the tip. Using a screwdriver, you drive this anchor in without predrilling; when the head nears the wall, two short wings on the plastic shaft pull it flush to the surface. Next you insert the machine screw. As you do, the screw pushes the toggle sideways until the threads on the screw engage the threads on the toggle. Then you tighten the screw until the toggle is firmly drawn to the back of the drywall. This anchor is rated for 100 lb. in drywall.

PULL TOGGLES

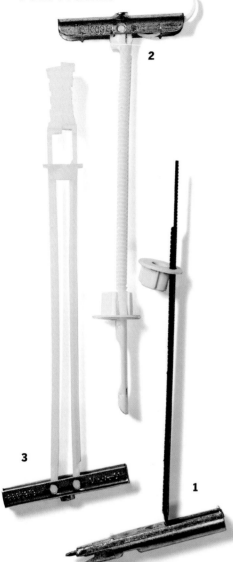

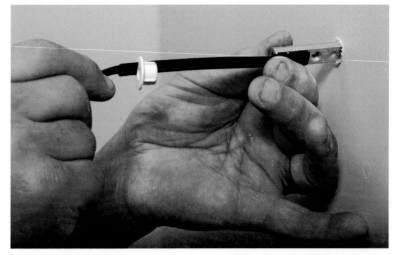

These are a new breed of toggle anchors that link a metal toggle with one or two ribbed plastic pull strips. After drilling a hole in a hollow wall, you insert the toggle and push it all the way through until it clears the hole. Next you pull on the strips until the toggle is crosswise and tight to the inside of the wall. Then, to keep the toggle in place, you slide a threaded plastic nut along the pull strip until it plugs into the hole you drilled. With the strips pulled tight, you bend them back and forth until they snap off flush with the nut. Now you can insert the machine screw; as the screw is tightened the toggle is pulled ever more firmly to the inside of the wall. These toggles will work with any hollow wall, from drywall and plaster to cinderblock.

The Hillman Pull Toggle (1), with a spiked, solid-metal toggle and a single pull strip, is rated for 120 lb. in drywall and 620 lb. in concrete block; the Cobra Flip Toggle (2), with a formed sheet metal toggle, is rated for 105 lb. in drywall and 435 lb. in block; the Toggler Snaptoggle (3) has two pull strips, both hinged to the toggle, and once you have inserted it you can use the strips to swivel the toggle so it is parallel to the back of the wall; it is rated 240 lb. in drywall and 800 lb. in concrete block.

Beyond drywall

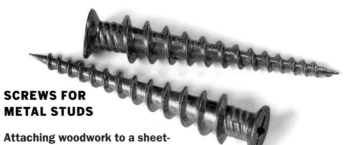

SCREWS FOR METAL STUDS

Attaching woodwork to a sheet-rock wall that has metal studs is not much different than doing so on a wall with wood studs. Any of the drywall anchors mentioned here will work between the studs. And if the stud is in the right place, you can drive a long, heavy screw directly into it. But if you want to create a particularly strong anchor point right on the steel studs themselves, you could try 1Shot steel stud anchors, which are rated for 300 lb. when driven into a steel stud. You can use them like a giant screw to attach a workpiece to the wall, or you can use them like an anchor, driving them flush to the drywall and hanging the workpiece using a #8 screw driven into the hollow shank of the 1Shot.

SCREWS FOR MASONRY

Tapcon screws, or blue screws, have become a dependable favorite of mine for installing woodwork on a concrete or masonry wall. They let you skip masonry anchors and the big holes they require. These screws need only a small pilot hole (made with a masonry bit and a hammer drill) before being driven into place. With their unique double-threading, they possess the ability to tap their own threads in concrete or brick, so they hold fast. I live in an old house that still has brick behind plaster-on-lath party walls. In the correct length, Tapcon screws allow me to go right past the plaster and lath and into solid brick. I've never had a blue screw strip or had its head snap off.

You can buy Buildex Tapcon Concrete Anchors in star drive or Phillips-head versions, and they're available as a kit that comes with the correctly sized masonry bit.

EXPANDING MASONRY ANCHORS

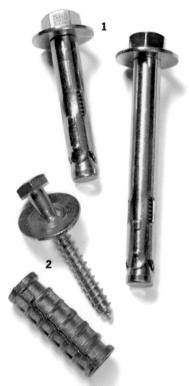

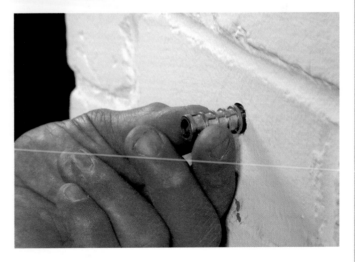

Red Head Sleeve Anchors (1) have a threaded bolt in a metal sleeve. One end of the bolt is flared, so that when a nut is tightened on the other end the wedge expands the sleeve, locking it in the hole. Wedge anchors require a hole drilled slightly deeper than the length of the anchor. After you drill the hole with a masonry bit and hammer drill, be sure to vacuum out the brick or cinder dust. Then slide the anchor into the hole. Once it's seated, the threaded portion of the anchor, extending from the wall, receives a washer and nut to secure the woodwork to the wall. They're a little unsightly, but very strong. Once the anchor is fixed into the masonry, the woodwork can be easily attached, adjusted, or removed without compromising the seated anchor.

When you want to attach with screws or lag screws, use lead sleeve anchors. These old-style Everbilt soft lead lag sleeves (2) are studded with projections and built in two loosely connected halves, allowing them to expand and shift in shape to conform to a predrilled hole when the screw is driven home.

Elegant Bookcase Top to Bottom

MIKE KORSAK

If you read and appreciate books, as I do, then you probably appreciate the functional aspects of a bookcase. If you enjoy beautiful materials and elegant, understated design, as I do, then I hope the design of this piece will appeal to you as well. I built it with a matched set of curly maple boards, which I purchased from Irion Lumber. I paired the maple with sexy, straight-grained bubinga for the base. And I used East Indian rosewood as an accent.

There is a lot of exacting joinery in the carcase, which has sliding dovetails joining the

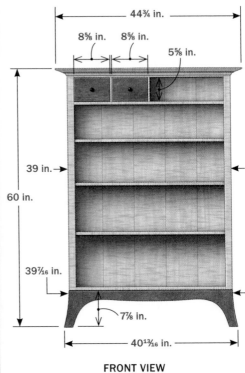

FRONT VIEW

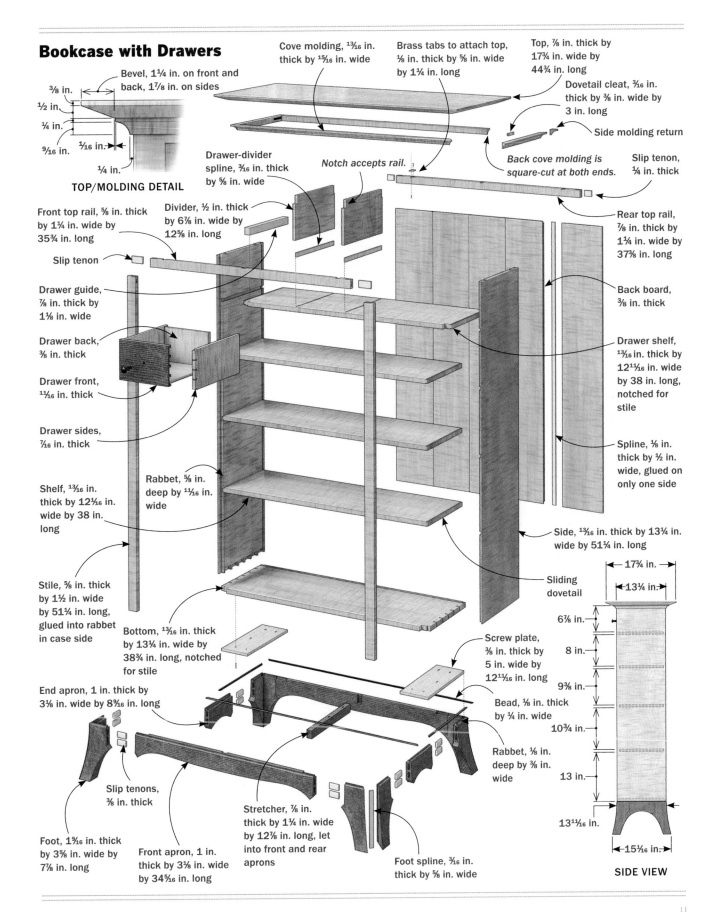

Bookcase with Drawers

Bevel, 1¼ in. on front and back, 1⅞ in. on sides

3⁄8 in.
½ in.
¼ in.
9⁄16 in.
1⁄16 in.
¼ in.

TOP/MOLDING DETAIL

Cove molding, 13⁄16 in. thick by 15⁄16 in. wide

Brass tabs to attach top, ⅛ in. thick by 5⁄8 in. wide by 1¼ in. long

Top, 7⁄8 in. thick by 17¾ in. wide by 44¾ in. long

Dovetail cleat, 3⁄16 in. thick by 3⁄8 in. wide by 3 in. long

Side molding return

Back cove molding is square-cut at both ends.

Slip tenon, ¼ in. thick

Drawer-divider spline, 3⁄16 in. thick by 5⁄8 in. wide

Notch accepts rail.

Divider, ½ in. thick by 6⅞ in. wide by 12⅝ in. long

Rear top rail, 7⁄8 in. thick by 1¼ in. wide by 37⅝ in. long

Front top rail, 5⁄8 in. thick by 1¼ in. wide by 35¾ in. long

Slip tenon

Back board, 3⁄8 in. thick

Drawer guide, 7⁄8 in. thick by 1⅛ in. wide

Drawer back, 3⁄8 in. thick

Drawer front, 11⁄16 in. thick

Drawer sides, 7⁄16 in. thick

Drawer shelf, 13⁄16 in. thick by 12 11⁄16 in. wide by 38 in. long, notched for stile

Spline, ⅛ in. thick by ½ in. wide, glued on only one side

Shelf, 13⁄16 in. thick by 12⅛ in. wide by 38 in. long

Rabbet, 5⁄8 in. deep by 11⁄16 in. wide

Side, 13⁄16 in. thick by 13¼ in. wide by 51¼ in. long

Sliding dovetail

Stile, 5⁄8 in. thick by 1½ in. wide by 51¼ in. long, glued into rabbet in case side

Bottom, 13⁄16 in. thick by 13¼ in. wide by 38¾ in. long, notched for stile

Screw plate, 3⁄8 in. thick by 5 in. wide by 12 11⁄16 in. long

End apron, 1 in. thick by 3⅛ in. wide by 8 9⁄16 in. long

Slip tenons, 3⁄8 in. thick

Bead, ⅛ in. thick by ¼ in. wide

Rabbet, ⅛ in. deep by 3⁄8 in. wide

Foot, 1 3⁄16 in. thick by 3⅝ in. wide by 7⅞ in. long

Front apron, 1 in. thick by 3⅛ in. wide by 34 5⁄16 in. long

Stretcher, 7⁄8 in. thick by 1¼ in. wide by 12⅞ in. long, let into front and rear aprons

Foot spline, 3⁄16 in. thick by 5⁄8 in. wide

SIDE VIEW

17¾ in.
13¼ in.
6⅞ in.
8 in.
9⅜ in.
10¾ in.
13 in.
13 11⁄16 in.
15 1⁄16 in.

Base detail.
The innocent-looking base is packed with curves and joinery.

shelves to the sides and half-blind dovetails joining the sides to the bottom. That's all spelled out in the drawing. But for this article I've chosen to focus on the base and the top molding. These two components might not be the first things to catch your eye, but they are vital to the look of the piece, and they are both a bit more challenging than they might seem.

Feet first

The feet on this base pack a lot of curves and unusual joinery into a small space. I begin making them by cutting the angled kerf for the gunstock miters. These little miters add a bit of refinement to the design and also

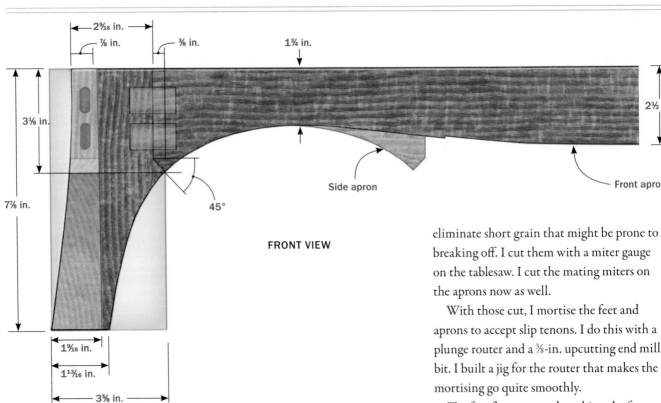

2⁹⁄₁₆ in.
⅞ in.
⅜ in.
1¾ in.
2½ in.
3⅛ in.
7⅞ in.
45°
Side apron
Front apron
1⁹⁄₁₆ in.
1¹³⁄₁₆ in.
3⅝ in.

FRONT VIEW

eliminate short grain that might be prone to breaking off. I cut them with a miter gauge on the tablesaw. I cut the mating miters on the aprons now as well.

With those cut, I mortise the feet and aprons to accept slip tenons. I do this with a plunge router and a ⅜-in. upcutting end mill bit. I built a jig for the router that makes the mortising go quite smoothly.

The feet flare outward, making the feet and aprons slightly concave on their outer faces. To create that flare, I make a curved template and trace it onto the feet. Then I use the bandsaw to cut the profile. I'll remove some of the bandsaw marks at this point

Canted kerf. The base joinery begins with a kerf cut in the foot blank at 45° for the gunstock miter.

Sliding jig for slip tenons. Korsak made a router jig that has a channel on the back that captures the router fence, steadying the cut.

Bandsaw the sweep. The face of the foot is bandsawn to a curve.

The feet meet in a miter. Korsak miters the feet at the tablesaw, cutting in several passes to reduce pressure on the short workpiece.

Slot for a spline. With the feet mitered and the fence moved to the other side of the blade, cut a groove for the spline.

Finish the gunstock. Korsak roughs out the shoulder on the bandsaw. He'll follow up with multiple crosscuts on the tablesaw.

Make the aprons. Korsak creates the slight concavity on the outer face of the apron with multiple passes at the tablesaw, adjusting the fence and the blade height with each pass.

7⁄8 in.

3 1⁄8 in.

1 in.

Complete the sweep. Having left some wood at the edge of the apron to support it as he cut the sweep, Korsak flips the board on edge to cut that wood away.

Cut the edge of the apron. Using relief cuts and entering from both ends in turn, Korsak carefully cuts out the curved edge of the apron.

Finish shaping the foot. With the sweep and the miter cut, bandsaw the foot's curved edge. It will get cleaned up after assembly.

with hand tools, but I wait until the base is fully assembled to finish the cleanup.

Next I cut the miters where the two halves of each foot are joined. I rip these miters on the tablesaw, with the blade set at 45°. Then, without changing the sawblade angle, I move the fence to the opposite side of the blade and cut spline grooves in the mitered faces.

Finish the joinery by bandsawing away the material above the gunstock miters. These cuts can be cleaned up using a crosscut sled at the tablesaw by nibbling across, taking multiple passes. Do final fitting with a block plane and chisel.

At this point I rough out the concave face of the aprons. First I dry-assemble each foot-to-apron joint and trace the curve of the foot onto the end grain of the apron. Then, at the tablesaw, I make multiple ripcuts to waste the bulk of the wood. Afterward, to fair the curve, I use a spokeshave with a convex sole.

Before moving on to assembly, I bandsaw the curved cutout along the edges of the feet and aprons. I leave a little extra material at the gunstock miter, where the transition from foot to apron occurs. I'll clean this up after assembly.

Assembling the base

Base assembly begins with gluing the foot-to-apron joints one at a time. After the subassemblies are glued up, I use a handplane to flush the tops of the feet to the tops of the aprons, and to ensure that the tops of the subassemblies are flat. I also mill a rabbet on the top to accept the decorative rosewood bead that punctuates the transition from base to case.

I take the time now to fine-tune the fit of the foot miters, using a block plane and dry-fitting each joint. With each joint dialed in, I pre-glue a spline into one of the feet at each corner joint. This saves valuable time during the glue-up, and ensures that the spline won't

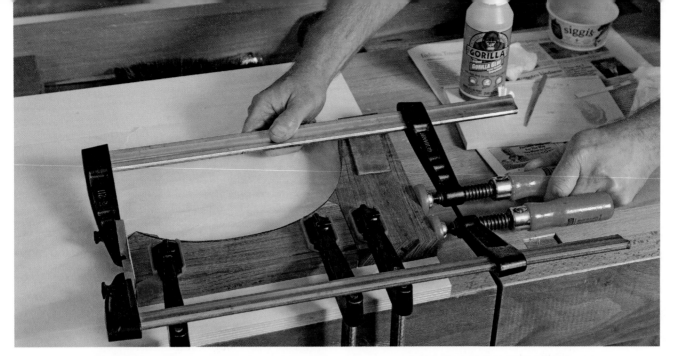

Start to assemble the base. Using a mitered cutoff as a caul to protect its vulnerable mitered edge, Korsak glues the foot to the apron.

Interrupt the assembly. After gluing feet to both ends of each apron, cut the rabbet where the decorative bead will be seated.

Excellent caul. Using cutoffs from shaping the foot, Korsak makes clamping cauls that fit its face and edge curves and enable him to exert pressure perpendicular to the miter joint.

Careful at the corners. Korsak glues up one corner of the base at a time for maximum control. For the last corner he separates the feet just enough to apply glue to the miter and spline.

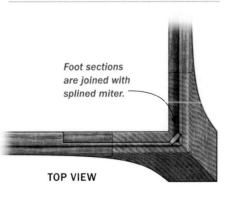

Foot sections are joined with splined miter.

TOP VIEW

shift and prevent the joint from pulling to-gether properly.

To help with the final glue-ups, I make custom clamping cauls using offcuts generated while making the feet. Each caul is made with two offcuts—one matching the concave face of the foot and one matching the curved edge. To those two pieces I add a block ripped at 45°, which lets me exert clamping pressure perpendicular to the miter joint. With so much attention on preparation, actually gluing the corner joints is fairly straightforward. I tackle them one at a time.

Beads make everything better

Before attaching the base to the carcase, make and install the rosewood bead. I shape the bead with a scratch stock, working on both edges of a wide blank. Then I rip them

Beads by hand. With a shopmade scratch stock, Korsak cuts beads on both edges of a wide rosewood workpiece.

Slit into strips. Cut the beads free at the bandsaw, then smooth the bandsawn face of the bead with a handplane.

Glue the beads into the rabbet. Korsak uses painter's tape to keep the beads in place as he fixes them with glue and brads.

Screws keep the base in place. Elongated clearance holes permit the case to move with the seasons.

Mount the Cove Molding

Side moldings are screwed and glued at the front end, but unglued at the back; the dovetail cleat holds them tight but lets the case side expand and contract with the seasons.

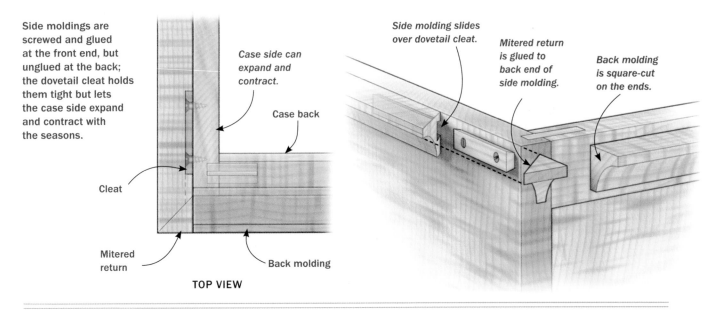

Case side can expand and contract.

Case back

Cleat

Mitered return

Back molding

TOP VIEW

Side molding slides over dovetail cleat.

Mitered return is glued to back end of side molding.

Back molding is square-cut on the ends.

Mitered molding. Having routed and scraped the cove molding to shape, Korsak miters it at the tablesaw. He keeps extra molding for setup later.

A socket in the back. Korsak routs a stopped socket in the back of the side molding to accept the dovetail cleat.

off the blank at the bandsaw and refine the bead with files and sandpaper. If I don't have stock long enough for the longest runs, I scarf shorter beads end-to-end.

I thoroughly enjoy installing the beads. Working with hand tools to cut and fit the miter and scarf joints is almost meditative, and the results are extremely rewarding. I drill pilot holes in the bead to prevent split-

ting, add a small amount of PVA glue, and fasten the bead with brads. I use glue sparingly, because squeeze-out around a bead can be difficult to remove.

Create the cove molding

Now it's on to the cove molding. I use blanks wide enough to yield two pieces of molding and shape the cove on the router

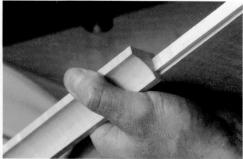

Cleat making. With the dovetail bit at the same height as for the socket, create cleat stock on an oversize blank. Korsak routs the cleat to a tight fit, then adjusts it with a plane. When the fit of the cleat is right, cut it off at the bandsaw.

table. To achieve a slightly elliptical cove with a round core-box bit, I nibble to the layout line by adjusting the bit depth and fence location for each pass. This leaves a ribbed profile, which I clean up with a curved card scraper followed by sandpaper. Then I rip the moldings to width.

The carcase is designed so the sides can expand and contract with the seasons. The cove moldings on the case sides have to permit this movement, so I fix them at the front end with screws and glue, but attach them at the back with sliding-dovetail cleats.

With my molding stock made, I miter both ends of the front piece and screw it in

place from inside the case. Then I cut and fit the mating miters on the front ends of the side molding pieces. I leave the back ends of the side moldings long for now. Next I mill a stopped dovetail socket in the back end of each side molding piece on the router table. I also mill a socket in a length of scrap molding.

To make the cleat stock, I reset the router fence and creep up on the size, using the scrap molding to check the fit. Then I rip the cleats off the blank and cut them to length (about 3 in.). To help install the cleats, I use the same piece of scrap molding. Cut to about 4 in. long, notched and drilled with two access holes, this scrap is now a jig for accurately locating, drilling out, and screwing in the cleats.

With the cleats installed, unscrew the front molding, slide the side moldings onto the cleats, and then reattach the front molding. Check the fit of the miters, then mark

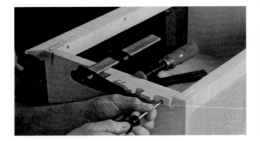

Invaluable scrap. A piece of scrap molding with a dovetail socket guides attachment of the cleat. Clamp the scrap flush to the top of the case, slide the cleat into the socket, and drill and screw it into place.

Fixed at the front. The side molding is screwed and glued at the front end, but not at the back, where it is held tight to the case by the cleat.

Tiny return. Because of the seasonal movement of the case sides, the side molding can't be joined to the back molding. For a clean seam, Korsak glues tiny mitered returns to the back end of the side molding.

Slide on the side molding. Having already cut and fitted the front miters on the side molding, Korsak unscrews the front molding and slides the side molding onto the cleat to mark for the rear miters.

the back ends of the side moldings for length. After cutting the back miters and reinstalling the moldings, glue on a mitered return at the back end. This will mate with (but not be joined to) the back molding. Once the cove molding is complete, attach the top and start thinking about filling this case with books.

Arts & Crafts Bookcase

WILLIE SANDRY

I like to build in the Arts and Crafts style, and I usually design each piece from the ground up. But once in a great while, I stumble onto a design that cannot be improved. This was the case with Charles P. Limbert's No. 355 Cottage Bookcase. With its glass doors and pierced panels featuring integral corbels, it's a true gem among Arts and Crafts designs.

Start with the sides

The No. 355 is like three small bookcases in one. There is a main case behind the glass door, flanked by two side-facing banks of open shelves. These side assemblies are the place to start. I use a pair of routing templates to make the pierced panels: one for the shelf dadoes and a second for the edge profile and cutouts.

Start with the dadoes for the shelves. I elected to make a full-size template and rout the dadoes using a guide bushing. The finished dadoes are ⅝ in. wide, so I use a ½-in.-dia. straight bit to cut them in two passes. I mount a ¾-in. guide bushing in the router that rides in ⅞-in.-wide slots in the template.

The next task is to rout the profile and the cutouts. I use a full-size template made from ½-in.-thick MDF that is longer than the workpiece. This extra length helps me to safely enter and exit the profile cut.

Use the template to mark the profile on the side panels. Then head over to the bandsaw and cut just outside the layout line. The two front panels receive the cutout, so you'll

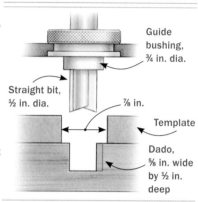

Rout the shelf dadoes. Clamp the dado template in place and use a router equipped with a straight bit and guide bushing to rout the dado in two passes.

Guide bushing, ¾ in. dia.

Straight bit, ½ in. dia.

⅞ in.

Template

Dado, ⅝ in. wide by ½ in. deep

A pair of templates for the sides. The pierced panels give the bookcase its unique look. Sandry uses one template for routing the shelf mortises and another for routing the profile and piercings.

Trace the profile and rough out the shape. Use the profile template to shape the panels. The front panels have a decorative cutout as well. Cut the profile at the bandsaw, staying just outside the line. Use a drill and jigsaw to remove the waste from the cutouts.

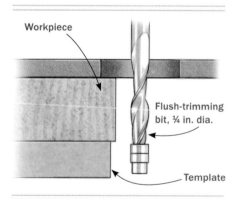

Workpiece

Flush-trimming bit, ¼ in. dia.

Template

Rout the profile. Clamp the profile template to the bottom of the panel. Then use a bearing-guided straight bit to rout the final shape. Work counterclockwise along the perimeter and clockwise around the inside of the cutout.

Limbert No. 355 Bookcase

Shelves on the sides of the case offer more storage space, while the pierced panels give the project its unique charm.

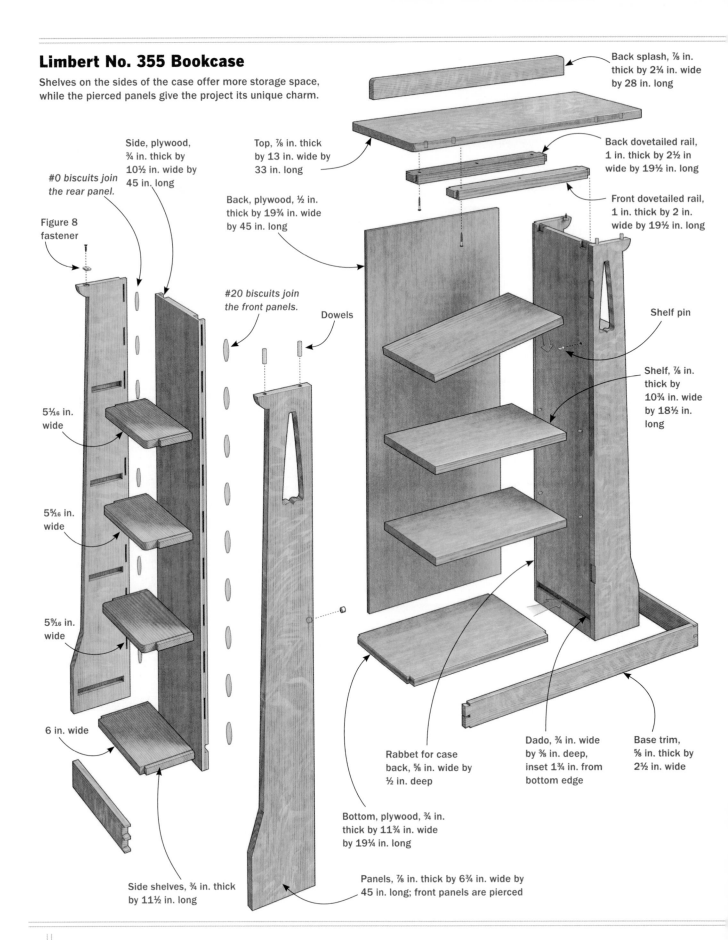

Back splash, ⅞ in. thick by 2¼ in. wide by 28 in. long

Side, plywood, ¾ in. thick by 10½ in. wide by 45 in. long

Top, ⅞ in. thick by 13 in. wide by 33 in. long

Back dovetailed rail, 1 in. thick by 2½ in wide by 19½ in. long

#0 biscuits join the rear panel.

Front dovetailed rail, 1 in. thick by 2 in. wide by 19½ in. long

Figure 8 fastener

Back, plywood, ½ in. thick by 19¾ in. wide by 45 in. long

#20 biscuits join the front panels.

Dowels

Shelf pin

Shelf, ⅞ in. thick by 10¾ in. wide by 18½ in. long

5¹⁄₁₆ in. wide

5⁵⁄₁₆ in. wide

5⁹⁄₁₆ in. wide

6 in. wide

Rabbet for case back, ⅝ in. wide by ½ in. deep

Dado, ¾ in. wide by ⅜ in. deep, inset 1¾ in. from bottom edge

Base trim, ⅝ in. thick by 2½ in. wide

Side shelves, ¾ in. thick by 11½ in. long

Bottom, plywood, ¾ in. thick by 11¾ in. wide by 19¼ in. long

Panels, ⅞ in. thick by 6¾ in. wide by 45 in. long; front panels are pierced

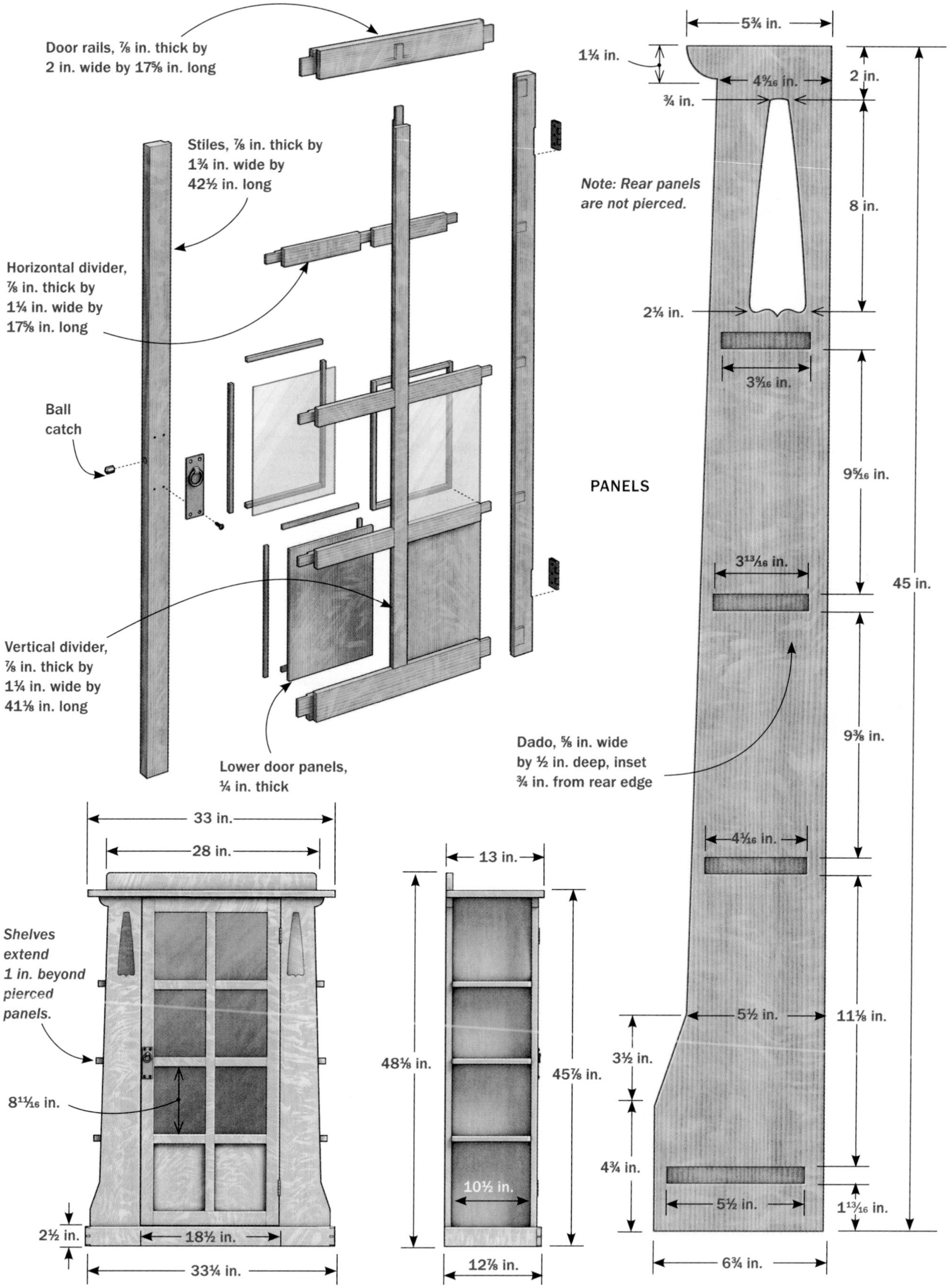

Door rails, ⅞ in. thick by 2 in. wide by 17⅝ in. long
Stiles, ⅞ in. thick by 1¾ in. wide by 42½ in. long
Horizontal divider, ⅞ in. thick by 1¼ in. wide by 17⅝ in. long
Ball catch
Vertical divider, ⅞ in. thick by 1¼ in. wide by 41⅛ in. long
Lower door panels, ¼ in. thick
5¾ in.
1¼ in.
4 9/16 in.
2 in.
¾ in.
Note: Rear panels are not pierced.
8 in.
2¼ in.
3 9/16 in.
PANELS
9 5/16 in.
3 13/16 in.
45 in.
9⅜ in.
Dado, ⅝ in. wide by ½ in. deep, inset ¾ in. from rear edge
4 1/16 in.
5½ in.
11⅛ in.
3½ in.
4¾ in.
5½ in.
1 13/16 in.
6¾ in.
33 in.
28 in.
Shelves extend 1 in. beyond pierced panels.
8 11/16 in.
2½ in.
18½ in.
33¼ in.
13 in.
48⅛ in.
45⅞ in.
10½ in.
12⅞ in.

A rabbet for the case back. Cut a rabbet in the rear face of just the rear panels. Use a dado blade buried in a sacrificial fence to make the cut in a single pass. Feed the stock with push pads to apply pressure along the cut for a rabbet of consistent depth.

Biscuits for the case side. Mark centerlines for the biscuits on both the panels and the case side. Register the base of the biscuit joiner on the tabletop to make the cuts in each part (above center). Finally, dado the inside face of the case sides (above) to accept the case bottom.

need to drill a hole and rough out the shape with a jigsaw.

Next, clamp the template to the panel, and then clamp both to the workbench. Make sure the panel is accurately positioned on your layout marks and trim it to shape with a router and flush-trimming bit. Because the grain direction changes along the profile, I use a ¼-in.-dia. down-cut spiral bit, which is ideal for handling the details and inside curves. Move the router in a counterclockwise direction along the edge of the panel and in a clockwise direction inside the cutout. Consider an oversize router baseplate for improved stability.

Now is a good time to circle back to the rabbets in the rear panels. These ½-in.-deep by ⅝-in.-wide rabbets receive the back of the center bookcase. Since the rabbets extend the entire length of the rear panel, they are easily handled with a dado blade at the tablesaw.

Then adjust the width of the dado stack to fit the ¾-in. plywood bottom of the center case and cut the dadoes for it on the inside face of the sides. It's important to position these dadoes accurately, so the case bottom aligns with the bottom side shelves.

Finally, tenon the side shelves to fit the dadoes in the front and rear panels. The upper three shelves extend beyond the panels and need rounded corners as well.

Glue the side units

When dry-fitting one of the side assemblies, I realized it was rather difficult to align the case side with the rear edge of the panels, while at the same time positioning the shelves correctly. The solution was a row of biscuits connecting the panels to the case side. I used #20 biscuits on the front pierced panel, and smaller #0 biscuits on the rear panel because of the rabbet along the edge.

Before assembly, do a complete dry-fitting and make sure all the components fit as they

Glue up the side assemblies, then connect them with the case bottom. Fit the case side and shelves into one panel and drop the second into place (above). Tap the shelves tight to the case side and clamp the assembly together. When dry, glue the side assemblies to the case bottom (above right).

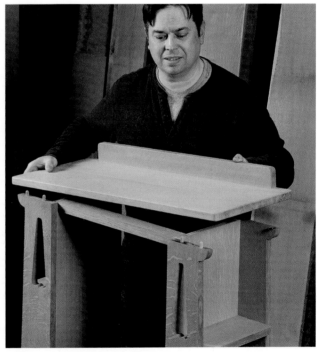

Add the dovetailed rails. A shallow rabbet on the bottom of the dovetail makes it easier to align the rail for scribing. After scribing, rout out the waste with a spiral bit and chisel into the corners. Then glue in the rails.

Finally, install the top. Glue the backsplash to the top, then screw the top to the case. Dowels align the top at the front edge. Glue the top only at the front and use figure-8 clips to secure it at the back to allow for wood movement.

A Frame with a Built-in Rabbet

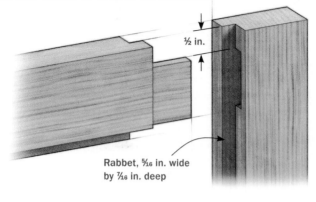

½ in.

Rabbet, ⁵⁄₁₆ in. wide
by ⁷⁄₁₆ in. deep

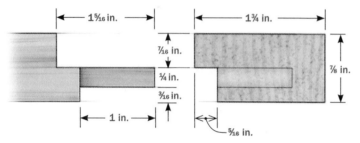

1⁵⁄₁₆ in.

1¾ in.

⁷⁄₁₆ in.

¼ in.

³⁄₁₆ in.

7/8 in.

1 in.

⁵⁄₁₆ in.

Making a divided-light door. While the joinery looks complex, it can all be handled easily at the tablesaw. Start with the rabbet. Use a dado blade partially buried in a sacrificial fence to make the cut.

Cut the front tenon cheek. Adjust the fence to the final width of the tenon and use a miter gauge to cut the cheek in two passes.

should. Once you're satisfied with all the joinery, you're ready for glue.

Apply glue to the dadoes and biscuit slots and assemble the side units. Make sure the case sides are flush with the top of the panels. While no glue is required behind the shelves, double check that there's no gap between the case side and shelves. Apply a small army of clamps and set the assemblies aside to dry for 24 hours.

Connect the side assemblies

Once the clamps are removed from the side assemblies, you can add the case bottom. You'll need to notch the corners of the bottom to fit the dadoes, which is an easy matter at the bandsaw. Give the bottom a good sanding and glue it between the two side assemblies. At this point the bookcase is starting to take shape.

Now move on to making the dovetailed rails that hold the bookshelf together at the top. Not only do they prevent splay at the top of the case, but they also function as a stop for the glass door, and firmly support the back of the case.

Determine the exact shoulder-to-shoulder length of the rails by measuring directly from the case sides. Cut a shoulder on the bottom of the rails to aid in alignment when scribing and dovetail the ends with a handsaw or at the bandsaw (see the bottom left photo on p. 45).

When scribing the case sides for the dovetails, set the front rail ⅛ in. back from the rear of the front panels to allow for a cork door bumper. Use a ¼-in.-dia. spiral bit and plunge router to excavate most of the waste, then use a sharp chisel to clean up the inside corners. Before gluing the rails in place, drill the countersunk holes in them that will be used to attach the top.

Cut the rear cheek. Adjust the fence to account for the width of the rabbet when cutting the second cheek.

Final assembly

There are a few loose ends to wrap up before this bookcase is finished. Install base trim along the front and sides of the case to tie everything together. The original piece featured a mitered molding, but I used dovetails at the corners instead. The shoulder-to-shoulder length on the face trim needs to be spot-on. The side trim pieces can be left long while dry-fitting the dovetail joints, and then marked and cut to length before final assembly.

Now move on to installing the top of the bookcase (see the bottom right photo on p. 45). Start by gluing the backsplash to the top, and then attach them as a unit. Dowels are used to align the top at the front of the case. Add glue and screw the top along the front rail. At the back, skip the glue and screw the top to the rear rail through elongated holes to allow for seasonal movement. Use figure-8 fasteners to secure the corners of the top to the rear panels.

Build the door

While you could assemble the door first and then rout a rabbet for the glass afterward, I like to make a door with a built-in rabbet (see drawing on facing page). The key is to rabbet the parts first, and then offset the tenon shoulders to match. This technique may seem daunting, but if taken one step at a time, it's not that difficult. And it saves you from squaring 32 inside corners.

Begin by rabbeting all the door parts. The horizontal and vertical dividers receive rabbets along both rear edges. Next, cut the mortises so they are aligned with the inside face of the rabbet. I cut them with a mortising machine, but any method would work. Then move on to the tenons, cutting them using a dado blade at the tablesaw. Start with the front cheek of the tenons, then adjust the fence to account for the width of the rabbet and cut the rear cheeks (see photos on the facing page and above). The result is a tenon with offset shoulders. Sneak up on the blade height until the tenon fits the mortise. Then incrementally adjust the rip fence until the offset shoulders seat fully in the rabbeted stiles.

The last bits of joinery for the door are half-laps on the dividers. Start with a 5/8-in.-wide dado stack and cut three half-laps in the back side of the vertical divider. Before you cut them, make a test cut in some scrap to confirm that a full 5/8-in. dado stack will make the cut in one pass (I had to add a 0.020-in. shim for the parts to fit), and set the blade height to match the rabbet.

Where the Dividers Meet (Rear View)

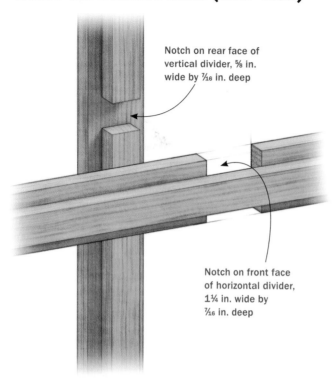

Notch on rear face of vertical divider, ⅝ in. wide by ⁷⁄₁₆ in. deep

Notch on front face of horizontal divider, 1¼ in. wide by ⁷⁄₁₆ in. deep

Notch the rear face of the vertical divider. Adjust the dado set to the width of the narrow portion of the divider and set the blade height equal to the rabbet. Register the divider end against the rip fence.

Notch the front face of the horizontal dividers. The wider notch will require two or more passes. Register the end of the divider against the rip fence for the first cut, then rotate it for the second cut. Using this technique will keep the notch centered.

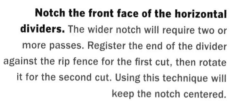

Bring it all together. To assemble the door, first connect the horizontal and vertical dividers (above). Then insert the assembly into the rails and finally add the stiles (right).

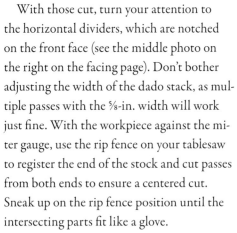

A simply beautiful finish. Sandry adds an overall tone to the wood by wiping on TransTint golden brown dye (above center). Then he seals the finish with SealCoat, a blond dewaxed shellac (above).

Add a glaze. Sandry uses General Finishes walnut gel stain as a glaze to darken the pores and highlight the medullary rays of the oak. He works the stain into the wood, then wipes it off to achieve the desired color. Sandry sealed it with a sprayed lacquer, but any satin finish would be appropriate.

With those cut, turn your attention to the horizontal dividers, which are notched on the front face (see the middle photo on the right on the facing page). Don't bother adjusting the width of the dado stack, as multiple passes with the ⅝-in. width will work just fine. With the workpiece against the miter gauge, use the rip fence on your tablesaw to register the end of the stock and cut passes from both ends to ensure a centered cut. Sneak up on the rip fence position until the intersecting parts fit like a glove.

Make glass stops to secure the individual panes in the door. This ⁵⁄₁₆ in.-square trim can be left extralong and cut to length after finishing. You will also need ⁵⁄₁₆-in. by ³⁄₁₆-in.

trim to secure the wooden panels in the door. After the finish is applied, attach the glass stops with a 23-gauge pin nailer and ⅝-in.-long pins, or dabs of silicone. I selected "hand blown" glass, which has slight wavy imperfections and occasional seedy texture.

Apply the finish

I used a stain-over-dye technique to highlight the medullary rays of the white

oak. After finish-sanding, raise the grain with a spray bottle of distilled water. Once the surface is dry, scuff-sand it with 220-grit sandpaper to knock down the raised grain. A final cleaning with cheesecloth and compressed air prepares the project for the first layer of color.

Next apply a water-based dye. In this case, I used TransTint golden brown mixed in a ratio of 1 oz. of dye to 1 qt. of distilled water. Apply the dye with a rag or staining sponge, moving quickly for consistent color. Follow that with a seal coat of shellac and finally a walnut gel stain used as a glaze. Sealing with a coat of shellac first makes it easier to get uniform color with the glaze coat. Wipe off

the excess gel stain until you are satisfied with the color. I sprayed two coats of pre-catalyzed lacquer as a topcoat. Any finish would work, but pick one with a "satin" sheen for an authentic Arts and Crafts look. Extruded brass hardware is the final "tip of the cap" to Limbert's creation.

A Nightstand That Doubles as a Bookcase

MICHAEL CULLEN

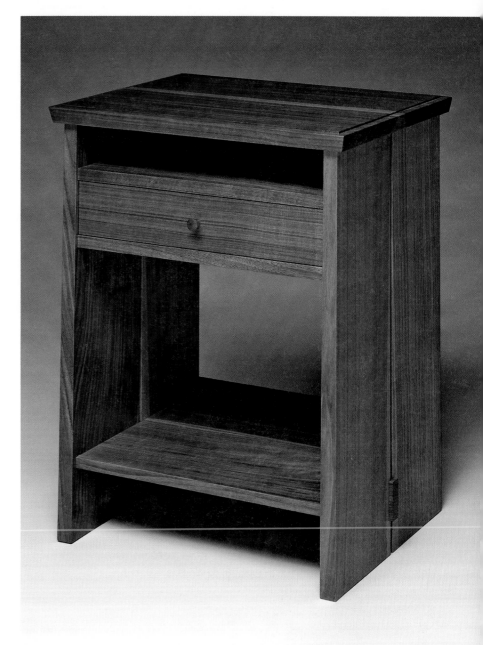

I designed this piece for a retired librarian who wanted a nightstand that would double as a bookcase. Of course it needed a drawer, which I sized to accommodate pencils and paper or an iPad, along with other items. Since so many essential things compete for space on the top of a nightstand—lamp, water glass, books and periodicals, alarm clock, eyeglasses—I decided to drop the drawer a few inches below the top, creating an easily reached space for the night's reading matter. Below the drawer I left ample room to store a collection of favorite books and magazines.

Even while juggling these functional considerations, I was sharply focused on the nightstand's form. The design is essentially rectilinear, but I didn't want it to read as blocky and plain.

Aiming to add visual interest and give the piece a subtly elegant presence, I made each side from a pair of boards with a narrow gap between them. I also tapered the sides slightly both in thickness and in width. I added a beveled, stepped detail around the top, and a stretcher beneath the lower shelf with tenons that protrude through the case sides.

The nightstand's primary joinery is a favorite of mine for solid-wood casework: the housed mortise-and-tenon. Between its full tenons the joint has stub tenons, or haunches, that tuck into a mating dado, or housing. This arrangement gives the joint maximum shear strength; keeps the tenoned

Stout Joinery and Sleek Lines

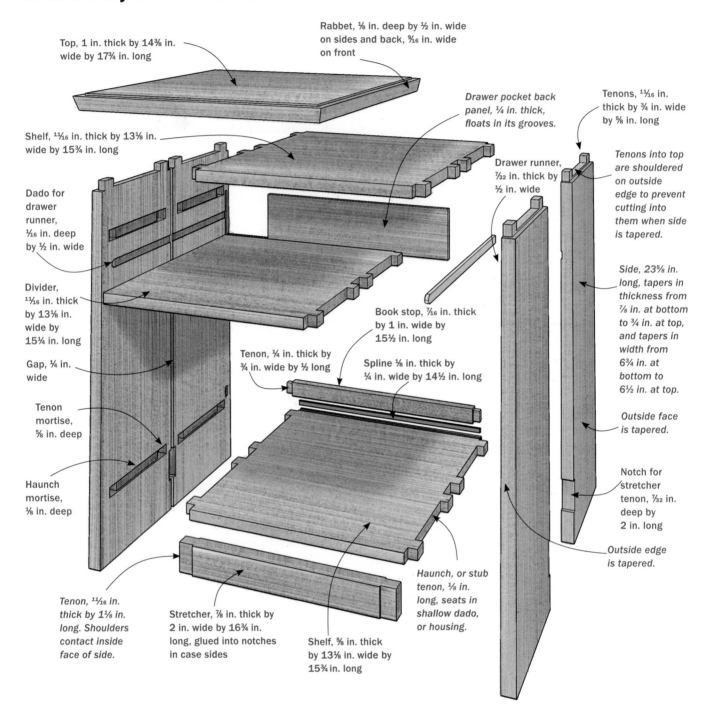

Top, 1 in. thick by 14⅜ in. wide by 17¾ in. long

Rabbet, ⅛ in. deep by ½ in. wide on sides and back, 9/16 in. wide on front

Drawer pocket back panel, ¼ in. thick, floats in its grooves.

Tenons, 11/16 in. thick by ¾ in. wide by ⅝ in. long

Tenons into top are shouldered on outside edge to prevent cutting into them when side is tapered.

Shelf, 11/16 in. thick by 13⅛ in. wide by 15¾ in. long

Drawer runner, 7/32 in. thick by ½ in. wide

Dado for drawer runner, 1/16 in. deep by ½ in. wide

Divider, 11/16 in. thick by 13⅛ in. wide by 15¼ in. long

Side, 23⅝ in. long, tapers in thickness from ⅞ in. at bottom to ¾ in. at top, and tapers in width from 6¾ in. at bottom to 6½ in. at top.

Gap, ¼ in. wide

Outside face is tapered.

Book stop, 7/16 in. thick by 1 in. wide by 15½ in. long

Tenon, ¼ in. thick by ¾ in. wide by ½ long

Spline ⅛ in. thick by ¼ in. wide by 14½ in. long

Tenon mortise, ⅝ in. deep

Notch for stretcher tenon, 7/32 in. deep by 2 in. long

Haunch mortise, ⅛ in. deep

Outside edge is tapered.

Tenon, 11/16 in. thick by 1⅛ in. long. Shoulders contact inside face of side.

Stretcher, ⅞ in. thick by 2 in. wide by 16¾ in. long, glued into notches in case sides

Shelf, ⅝ in. thick by 13⅛ in. wide by 15¾ in. long

Haunch, or stub tenon, ⅛ in. long, seats in shallow dado, or housing.

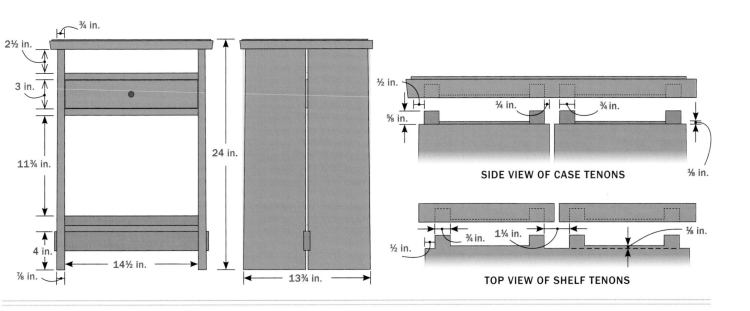

½ in.

¾ in.

2½ in.

3 in.

11¾ in.

24 in.

4 in.

⅞ in.

14½ in.

13¾ in.

SIDE VIEW OF CASE TENONS

½ in.

⅝ in.

¼ in.

¾ in.

⅛ in.

TOP VIEW OF SHELF TENONS

½ in.

¾ in.

1¼ in.

⅛ in.

Initial housed mortise-and-tenon layout.
Cullen lays out the full tenons and then the
haunch between them. He uses a marking
gauge for layout and a mechanical pencil to
clarify the lines.

member from warping; hides any small openings that develop over time; and, because it
has relatively small shoulders, makes it easier
to ensure a tight joint line. I learned the
housed tenon from my mentor, David Pow-
ell, at the school he ran in Massachusetts,
Leeds Design Workshops. I've relied on this
joint heavily over the years, and I think it's
unparalleled in soundness and strength.

Which wood?

I've made this nightstand a number of times,
and almost any hardwood—maple, cherry,
walnut, and oak, to name a few—would be
well suited for it, and certainly many exotics
as well. I've built one in wenge and another
in bubinga. This time I chose claro walnut,
taking all the parts from a single slab. As
with any piece of furniture, it's crucial to
match grain and color throughout the piece
to ensure visual balance. If you are building
a pair of nightstands, consider mirroring the
patterns of color and grain between the two.

Prepare the parts

I cut out all the nightstand parts slightly
oversize at the beginning of the project. This
way they have plenty of time to acclimate and
reach equilibrium in the workshop before
being brought to final size.

In preparation for laying out the housed
mortise-and-tenons, plane the sides to their
maximum thickness (⅞ in.) and cut them
to maximum width (6¾ in.). Then cut them
to length. You won't cut the tapers in the
sides' thickness or width until the joints are

Razor-Sharp Layout

Transfer the tenon locations from the horizontal members to the sides.

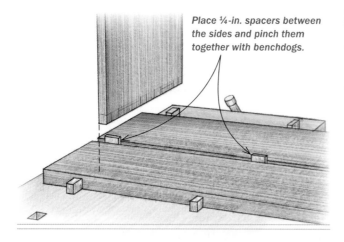

Place ¼-in. spacers between the sides and pinch them together with benchdogs.

Tenon transfer. Using an X-Acto knife for precision, Cullen transfers the tenon layout to the sides.

First drill, then chop. Using a Forstner bit in the drill press, Cullen removes most of the waste from the deep mortises. Then he uses a mallet and chisel to clean them up.

cut and fitted. The horizontal divider and the top and lower shelf should be milled to thickness and cut to size next. Be sure to leave them ever so slightly over thickness so you can sneak up on a perfect fit for the housed joints.

Begin layout with the tenons

The housed tenon joint calls for precise layout. All joinery should be scribed using a marking gauge and a sharp knife. I use an X-Acto. First lay out all the tenons—those on the horizontals and the ones at the top of the sides. To simplify the task, the tenons in the divider and the shelves should all be identically located. Four tenons per panel is ideal here. The tenons and haunches on the horizontal members are left the full thickness of the workpiece. But the tenons connecting the sides to the top are slightly different. Because the outside face of the sides will get tapered, you need a shoulder along the outside face. This way, the thickness of the tenons and the haunches will not change when the board is tapered.

Rout the housing. A router table makes quick work of cutting the housing for the haunch between tenons. Cullen uses a bit that's slightly under width and cuts the housing in two passes.

At this point I use the tenon layout on the horizontal members to lay out the mortises in the sides. Since the pair of boards that make up each side will be separated by ¼ in., I put ¼-in. spacers between them while making the transfer (see the drawing on the facing page). Although I've already laid out the tenons on the top of the sides, I don't lay out the mating mortises in the underside of the top just yet. I'll wait until all the other joinery is cut and I can dry-assemble the case and be absolutely sure of the tenons' location.

A jig for the cheeks. Cullen cuts the tenons to width on the tablesaw using his shopmade tenoning jig.

Make some mortises

I make the full mortises by drilling out the waste with a Forstner bit, then cleaning up with a mallet and chisel (see the center photo on the facing page). Alternately, you could rough out the mortises with a plunge router. Next I rout the dadoes for the haunched section of the joint. I cut these stopped dadoes at the router table, carefully lowering the workpiece onto the bit and using stop blocks to limit travel. The haunch, or stub tenon, will be ⅛ in. long, but make the dadoes slightly deeper than that. When the joint is closed, the three shouldered areas on the tenoned workpiece will contact the sides, but the haunches won't bottom out in the dadoes.

Bandsaw to the haunch line. A slightly rough end-grain cut on the haunch is fine, because it won't bottom out in the housing.

Chisel cleanup. Pare precisely to the baseline on the outside edges of the board and between the center tenons.

Tip for fitting. With the shelf still slightly over thickness, test the spacing of the mortises by tipping the workpiece. Then plane the faces of the board to achieve the final fit.

The stretcher needs notches. Several passes with a dado set on the tablesaw create one of the mating notches in the side that will accept the stretcher's tenon.

Fine-tune to fit. Before cutting the stretcher tenon's cheeks, Cullen planes the workpiece to width so it fits the notch exactly.

Shallow cheeks. After using the tenoning jig to shave the cheeks of the tenon, Cullen stays at the tablesaw but switches to the miter gauge to define the shoulders.

I prefer side-hung drawers, which require a shallow dado in the case side to house the drawer runner. That can be cut now (or after the tenons are cut) at the router table.

Take on the tenons

Once the mortises in the sides are complete, it's time to cut the tenons on the horizontal members. Use a tenoning jig on the tablesaw to cut the tenons to width, cutting right on the line (see the top photo on p. 55). Then use a miter gauge with a tall fence to cut the outside shoulders. I cut slightly to the waste side of the baseline and later clean up by paring with a chisel. After the tablesaw work is complete, bandsaw the waste from between the tenons, leaving a haunch ⅛ in. long. Between the center two tenons, bandsaw close to the baseline, then pare down to the line with a chisel.

Now it's time for the fun—getting the joint to fit and seat. Since the tenoned panel is still slightly over thickness, it's not going to fit the mortises completely. But you can check the side-to-side fit by lifting up the far end of the board and inserting a tip of the tenons into the mortises (bottom right photo p. 55). If necessary, return to the tablesaw to adjust the fit. The panel can then be carefully run through the planer to take off a whisper, or handplaned to fit using a sharp smoother. It's easy to go past the point of no return, so care and patience are essential. Plane the joints to a tight fit, and then finish-sand until the joint comes together snugly but with little effort. With such a complex assembly, you don't want much resistance when you apply the glue and pull the case together. The perfect dry-fit is one that just slides together and seats without any gaps.

More mortises

With most of the main joints cut and fitted, there are some smaller, simpler mortises to

Divider and top shelf get grooved. A dado head creates the ¼-in.-wide groove to receive the back panel of the drawer pocket.

Easy transfer. With the divider dry-fitted into the sides, transfer the location of the groove for the back panel.

Small router for a stopped groove. Cut the stopped groove for the back panel with a detail router fitted with a fence (above). The small mortise for the book stop's tenon (right) can be routed with the same setup used to cut the stopped groove for the back panel.

Create a shoulder, then the taper. The tenons at the top of the sides get shouldered on the outside face. This prevents the tenons from being altered when you taper the board's outside face.

cut. The ¼-in.-thick panel at the back of the drawer pocket is captured in four grooves. I cut through-grooves in the horizontal dividers at the tablesaw with a dado set. For the stopped grooves in the sides, I use a detail router with a ¼-in.-dia. bit and a clamped-on fence. I don't put any glue on the panel, and I leave a heavy ¹⁄₁₆-in. gap in the top groove to allow expansion of the panel.

The book stop at the back of the lower shelf gets tenoned into the sides and splined into the shelf. To cut the mortises for the book stop's tenons I again use the detail router, set up just as it was for the stopped grooves in the sides. For the spline groove—in both the book stop and the lower shelf—I use the tablesaw. Alternately, you could dispense with the spline and make a book stop with an integral tongue along its length that fits the groove in the shelf.

The final bit of joinery is for the stretcher that runs beneath the lower shelf and has proud through-tenons on each end. To make the "mortises" for the stretcher's tenons, cut mating notches in the sides using a miter gauge and a dado set on the tablesaw (see the top photo on p. 56). Refine the notches with a chisel. To cut the tenons, start by using a handplane to shave the width of the stretcher to a perfect fit. Then use the tenoning jig at the tablesaw for the cheeks and the miter gauge for the shoulders (see the bottom photo on p. 56).

Time to taper

The next step is to taper the sides. They taper ⅛ in. in thickness from bottom to top, and I use handplanes for this. I remove the bulk of the wood with my jointer plane, stopping just shy of the layout line. Then I perfect the surface with a smoothing plane, which will give me a surface ready for finish (see the top photo on the facing page). If I were making multiple nightstands, I might make

Inclined plane. Taper the sides using a jointer plane and working to layout lines on the edge of the workpiece. Switch to a smoothing plane to create the final surface.

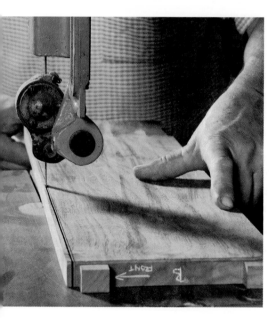

Taper number two. The cabinet sides are tapered in width as well as thickness. Make this angled cut on the bandsaw and clean it up with a handplane.

Last bit of layout. With the case dry-assembled, invert it and use the tenons to lay out the mortises in the top.

Exacting assembly. Having already sanded all the parts to 320-grit and applied an oil and wax finish, Cullen starts the glue-up (left) on a moving blanket. To protect the sides during clamping, Cullen made plywood cauls with cutouts for the proud stretcher tenons. When the case joints were clamped tight, he dry-fit the top and left it in place as the glue on the case joints dried.

a tapering jig for the planer, but for just one or two, tapering by hand is probably more efficient—and certainly more fun. To cut the taper in the width of the side, bandsaw to very near the layout line and smooth the edge with handplanes. Again, progress from a jointer to a smoother.

Getting to the glue-up

I sand and finish all the parts before assembly, which makes the finishing simpler and more consistent and prevents problems with glue squeeze-out. All the parts should be sanded to 320-grit, wiped down with a damp rag to raise the grain, and sanded again with 320-grit to prepare for the finish. I prefer a tung-oil finish for claro walnut followed by a light coat of wax. I use painter's tape to mask off the joinery so that no finish—and especially no wax—gets on the glue surfaces.

The lid is last. With the case cured, Cullen glues on the top. He uses narrow cauls to focus the clamping pressure directly above the cabinet sides.

This is a fairly complex glue-up and is best approached in two steps. First glue up the case with the top just dry-fitted. Then, when the glue cures, the top can be glued to the base. It's paramount in the first glue-up that everything is well thought out; the clamps and cauls should all be ready and the parts should be clearly labeled and set out. I find that the best time for a glue-up of this magnitude is early in the morning when my mind is clear and bright. About 15 or 20 minutes after each glue-up, check the piece for squeeze-out; the semi-dried glue should peel from the waxed wood surface.

Ship-Inspired Wall Shelf

CHRISTIAN BECKSVOORT

I have a thing for wall-mounted furnishings, be they clocks, lamps, cabinets, or shelves. The latest design is based on the mast and spars of a square-rigged sailing ship. It is designed to be light, graceful and strong, for display of books, DVDs, art objects, or just your collection of knickknacks. The whole shelf is designed to hang on a single stud. Like the spars on a ship, the shelves get thinner and smaller as they go farther up the rib.

Start with the center rib

All of the shelves branch out from the center rib (or mast). Before the rib has been tapered, and while both edges are still square and parallel, I cut the ⅛-in.-deep dadoes to hold all the shelves. That way I can flip the board to cut dadoes on both sides. Because the shelves go from thinner at the top to thicker at the bottom, all but two of the dadoes are of different widths. Cutting them is an organizational challenge. There is a lot of adding and subtracting spacers from the dado setup. Patience pays.

Once the dadoes are cut, the rib can be tapered, from 7½ in. at the largest shelf to about 1 in. at the top and bottom. I do this on the bandsaw, and then I clean up that cut at the bench with a handplane. The section above the top shelf is then gently tapered on both sides, to about ½ in. thick at the tip, again at the bench with handplanes.

Wall Shelf

While this shelf has a straightforward design, the graduated dimensions will keep you on your toes. The design remains light and airy because the shelves and their supports vary in thickness, depth, and length. Stay organized and you'll do fine.

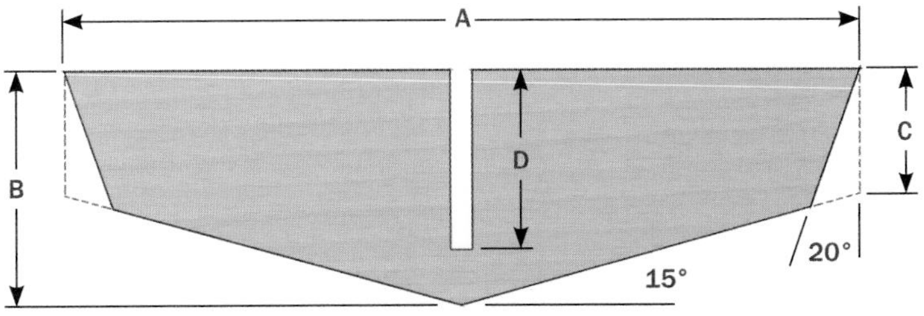
A
B
C
D
20°
15°

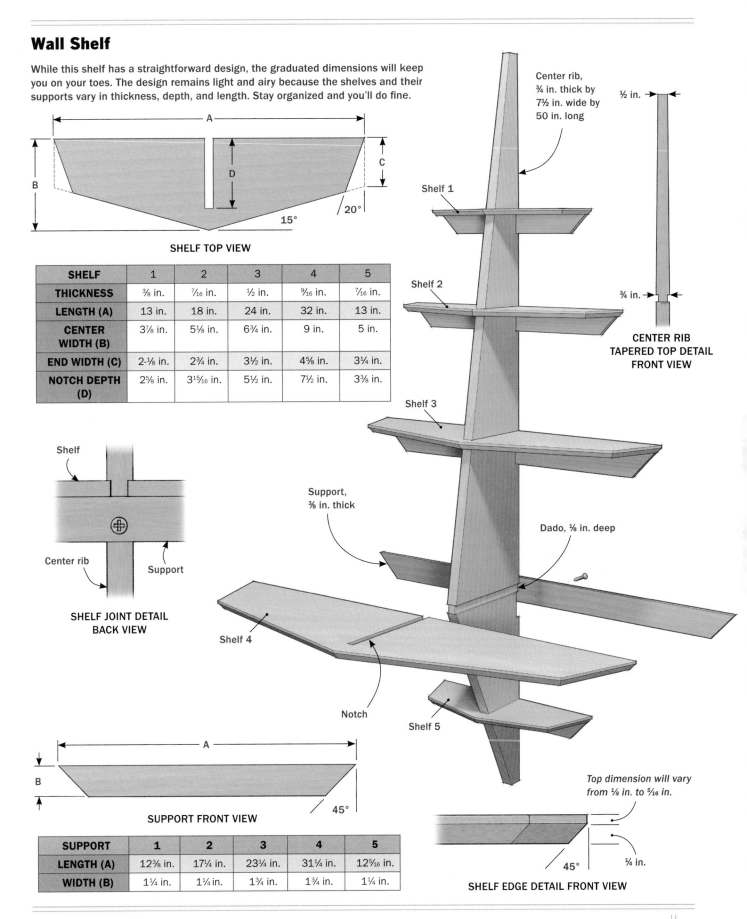

SHELF TOP VIEW

SHELF	1	2	3	4	5
THICKNESS	3/8 in.	7/16 in.	1/2 in.	9/16 in.	7/16 in.
LENGTH (A)	13 in.	18 in.	24 in.	32 in.	13 in.
CENTER WIDTH (B)	3 7/8 in.	5 1/8 in.	6 3/4 in.	9 in.	5 in.
END WIDTH (C)	2-1/8 in.	2 3/4 in.	3 1/2 in.	4 5/8 in.	3 1/4 in.
NOTCH DEPTH (D)	2 5/8 in.	3 15/16 in.	5 1/2 in.	7 1/2 in.	3 3/8 in.

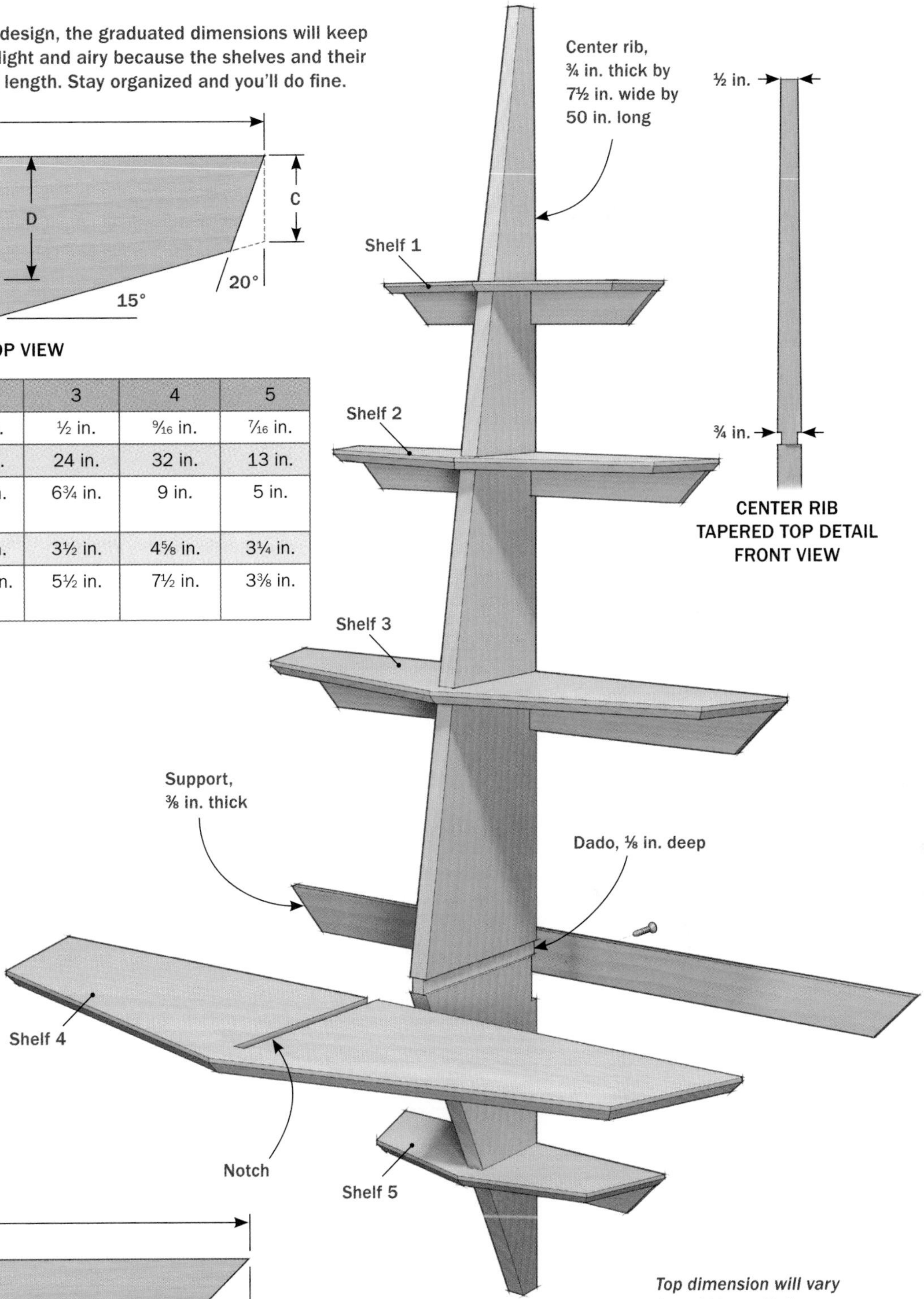
Center rib,
3/4 in. thick by
7 1/2 in. wide by
50 in. long
Shelf 1
Shelf 2
Shelf 3
Support,
3/8 in. thick
Dado, 1/8 in. deep
Shelf 4
Notch
Shelf 5
1/2 in.
3/4 in.

CENTER RIB
TAPERED TOP DETAIL
FRONT VIEW

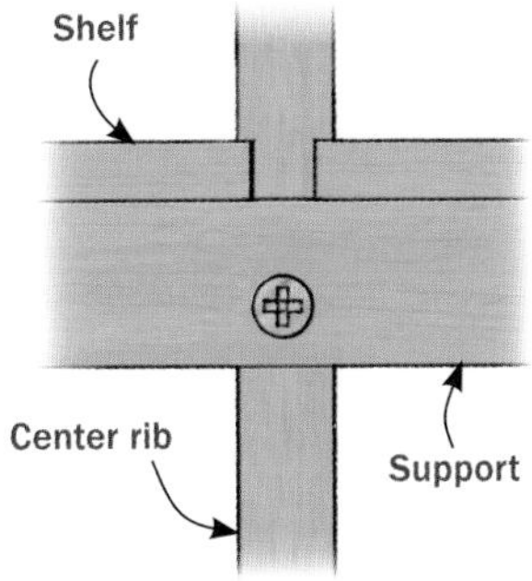
Shelf
Center rib
Support

SHELF JOINT DETAIL
BACK VIEW

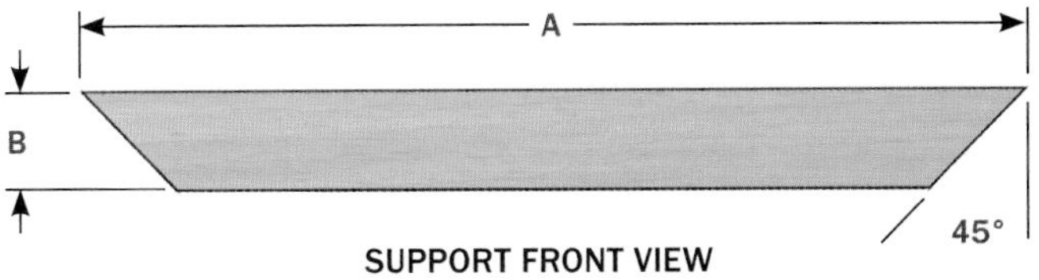
A
B
45°

SUPPORT FRONT VIEW

SUPPORT	1	2	3	4	5
LENGTH (A)	12 3/8 in.	17 1/4 in.	23 1/4 in.	31 1/4 in.	12 5/16 in.
WIDTH (B)	1 1/4 in.	1 1/4 in.	1 3/4 in.	1 3/4 in.	1 1/4 in.

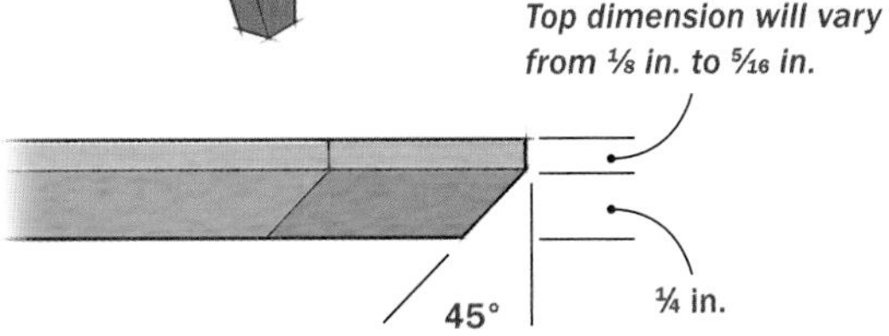
Top dimension will vary from 1/8 in. to 5/16 in.
45°
1/4 in.

SHELF EDGE DETAIL FRONT VIEW

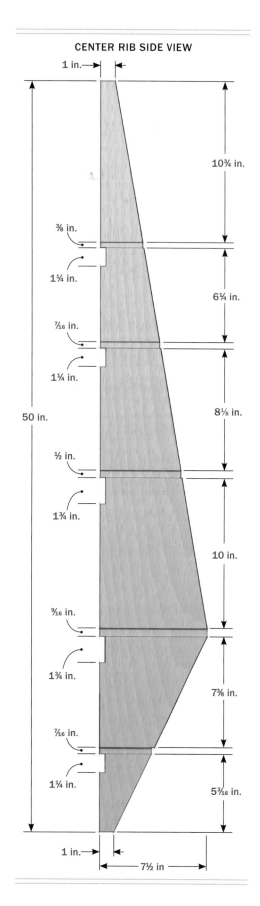

CENTER RIB SIDE VIEW

1 in.

10¾ in.

⅜ in.

1¼ in.

6¼ in.

⁷⁄₁₆ in.

1¼ in.

8⅛ in.

50 in.

½ in.

1¾ in.

10 in.

⁹⁄₁₆ in.

1¾ in.

7⅜ in.

⁷⁄₁₆ in.

1¼ in.

5³⁄₁₆ in.

1 in.

7½ in

Everything sticks to your rib. The main rib is the infrastructure that locks the shelves and shelf supports in place. Because the shelves gradually get thinner toward the top, there are a lot of dado blade changes to accommodate the different shelf thicknesses. Cut all these dadoes before you shape the rib.

Five different shelves

Next I cut the shelves. These are all different lengths, widths, and thicknesses. The extra effort to do this contributes to the grace of the piece. It would be very clunky if everything had the same dimensions. Once the shelf blanks are milled, I locate the center and cut a ½-in. slot to fit and correspond to the dadoes cut into the center rib. Then I taper each shelf on the bandsaw from the center to both ends. I also cut a 20° angle on the ends. Finally, to make the shelves look even lighter, I rout the undersides of the three visible edges at 45°.

Shelf supports add strength

The shelf supports are next. Like the shelves, they vary in size, though all are ⅜ in. thick. The supports for the two large shelves are

Shape the rib. On the bandsaw, the front of the rib gets tapered in two directions. After cutting the tapers, Becksvoort smooths the bandsawn edges at the bench with a handplane.

Square the front at the dadoes. With a chisel, create a shoulder connecting the two dadoes, cutting the front edge of the rib parallel to the back edge. This will allow the shelf to be inserted fully so it sits flush with the back of the rib.

Thickness the shelves, starting at the planer.
Keep the dadoed rib close at hand so you can test each shelf in its dado. Start by planing the thickest shelf and work your way down to the thinnest one. The five shelves are of varying widths and thicknesses. Patience and organization will help you keep track of what you're doing where.

1¾ in. wide, while the three smaller shelves have 1¼-in.-wide supports. To lay out the notches in the rib that accept the supports, slide the shelves temporarily in place. Hold a support under its shelf in the back, making sure it is perfectly flush with the shelf. Then mark the width on the back of the rib. Repeat for all five shelves, remove the shelves, and with the dado blade set to ⅜ in. high, cut from each mark up to the dado. Dry-fit all 11 pieces together and mark the supports where they meet the 45° undercut on the shelves. Then cut the supports to length.

Notch and shape the shelves. Locate the center point, and cut a ½-in. notch that will slot into the dadoes in the rib (1). On the bandsaw, cut the tapers on the fronts of the shelves (2). Then move to the tablesaw to cut the angles on the ends (3). Finally, use a handsaw to extend the saw line and then a chisel to square the end of the notch (4).

Glue up shelf by shelf, then add hangers and finish

Sand all the parts and glue the shelves into their dadoes. Then add a thin layer of glue on the tops of the supports and in the notches for them and slide the supports under the shelves. Clamp with spring clamps.

Once the glue is dry and the clamps are off, turn the shelf over onto its face and rout and drill for two cabinet hangers on the back of the center rib between the first and second shelves and the third and fourth shelves.

I finish my shelf with a mix of two parts Tried & True varnish oil mixed with about one part spar varnish. I apply three coats with a good 0000 steel wool rub between coats.

To hang the shelf, locate a wall stud with a magnet or stud finder. Place a strip of ¾-in.

Mark and notch for the support. The shelves are designed to radiate from one vertical point, the rib. To make it structurally sound you must beef up the shelves with supports that are notched into the rib, locking it all together. With a shelf slotted partway onto the rib and the support butted against the shelf, use a knife to mark the width of the support (top). At the tablesaw, use a dado blade to cut the notches in the rib (above).

blue tape exactly over the stud, making sure the tape is perfectly plumb. Put two ⅜-in. dowel centers in the hanger holes and press the shelf onto the blue tape, being sure that the rib is plumb. Remove the tape and screw two screws (minimum length 2 in.) into the dimples left by the dowel centers, so that there is only about ⅛ in. of screw shaft between the wall and the screw head. Hang your shelf, decorate it, and stand back and admire your work.

One shelf, five separate glue-ups. Working on one shelf at a time, apply glue to the dado and slide the shelf all the way into place. Then add glue to the top edge of the support and to the notch, and clamp the support to the shelf with spring clamps. Drive a predrilled, countersunk screw through the support into the rib (below).

Rout and install. This shelf hangs on two keyhole hangers in one plane on the rib. Each keyhole hanger requires a stepped mortise (top). The shallow outer mortise lets the hardware sit flush with the surface of the wood or just a hair below. The deep inner one accepts the screw head.

Locate and hang. Becksvoort finds the wall stud and marks it with a strip of blue tape. If you aren't using a stud, be sure to use wall anchors that are strong enough to support the shelf and its contents. With dowel center markers in the keyhole hangers, press the shelf in place on the blue tape. The dowel centers will mark the tape and the drywall underneath for the precise placement of your screws.

Modern Wall Shelf

CHRISTIAN BECKSVOORT

One of the reasons I like the Shaker style is because Shakers seldom followed traditional rules of design. The golden mean went out the window, while function was the overriding design element. They favored the tall and narrow and embraced asymmetrical layout.

When contemplating a wall shelf unit, I decided to incorporate the long, skinny, asymmetrical look into my design. I wanted something out of the ordinary, yet graceful and functional. After a series of brainstorm sketches, I came up with this version with two vertical uprights, two long, unaligned horizontal shelves, and two suspended drawers. To lighten things up I chamfered the ends of the shelves.

Four case parts with simple, smart joinery

I placed the uprights 32 in. apart on center so that the shelf can be mounted to studs on plaster walls or drywall. If you aren't hitting studs when you mount this shelf on the wall, you'll have to use some type of wall anchor with the screws.

The intersections of the vertical and horizontal elements in this shelf are merely lap joints, with shallow dadoes cut into both sides of the uprights. The dadoes help to align the parts and support the shelves. The dadoes and lap joints can be cut either on the tablesaw or by hand. I use a combination of both. I cut the dadoes first on the tablesaw. Then I do a stopped cut, also on the tablesaw, to get the lap joints cut. These I clean square with a handsaw and chisel. I cut the laps into the front halves of the shelves and the back halves of the uprights. Since the shelves are offset in opposite directions, the laps are in opposite locations on the shelves.

70

Wall Shelf

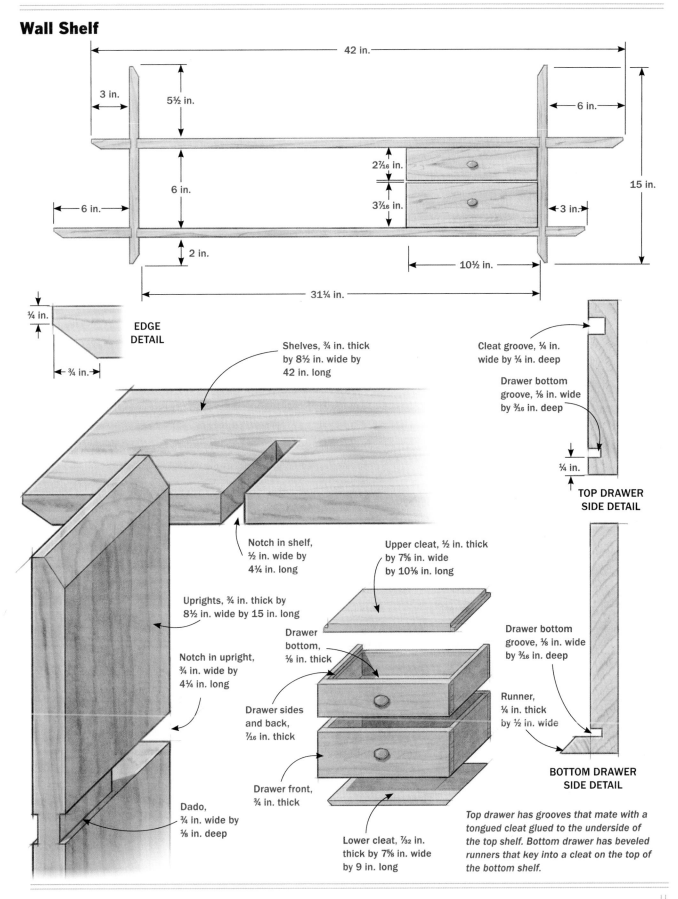

42 in.

3 in.

5½ in.

6 in.

6 in.

6 in.

2 in.

31¼ in.

2⁷⁄₁₆ in.

3⁷⁄₁₆ in.

10½ in.

3 in.

15 in.

¼ in.

¾ in.

EDGE DETAIL

Shelves, ¾ in. thick by 8½ in. wide by 42 in. long

Notch in shelf, ½ in. wide by 4¼ in. long

Uprights, ¾ in. thick by 8½ in. wide by 15 in. long

Notch in upright, ¾ in. wide by 4¼ in. long

Dado, ¾ in. wide by ⅛ in. deep

Drawer bottom, ⅛ in. thick

Drawer sides and back, ⁷⁄₁₆ in. thick

Drawer front, ¾ in. thick

Lower cleat, ⁷⁄₃₂ in. thick by 7⅝ in. wide by 9 in. long

Upper cleat, ½ in. thick by 7⅝ in. wide by 10⅛ in. long

Cleat groove, ¼ in. wide by ¼ in. deep

Drawer bottom groove, ⅛ in. wide by ³⁄₁₆ in. deep

¼ in.

TOP DRAWER SIDE DETAIL

Drawer bottom groove, ⅛ in. wide by ³⁄₁₆ in. deep

Runner, ¼ in. thick by ½ in. wide

BOTTOM DRAWER SIDE DETAIL

Top drawer has grooves that mate with a tongued cleat glued to the underside of the top shelf. Bottom drawer has beveled runners that key into a cleat on the top of the bottom shelf.

The uprights get dadoes and a lap joint. On the tablesaw with a miter gauge, cut the shallow dadoes first. Then, without moving the fence, cut the lap joint in the same place as the dado. Use a stop on the fence to keep you from cutting too far.

The shelves get just a lap. Set the dado blade for a ½-in.-wide kerf and cut the notch in the shelf for the lap. The laps are not equidistant from the ends so you'll need to adjust the rip fence for the second cut.

Chisel to the centerline.

Stopped sawcut

Clean up the lap joint by hand. Use a handsaw to extend the lap to the centerline. Then chisel it square.

A quick and easy glue-up. Becksvoort applies glue in the dadoes, pieces the two vertical and two horizontal pieces together, and applies clamp pressure.

Back it up with a screw. To add extra strength to the bottom joint, drill and then drive a screw into the back edge of the upright just above the bottom shelf, through the shelf, and into the 2-in. section below.

Add hangers for solid support. A keyhole hanger, mortised into the upright, straddles the upper shelf, helping shore up construction. Becksvoort uses a 3-in. Rockler double keyhole fitting, item no. 28829.

Scribe around the hanger. Position the hanger on the upright. If you're using the double keyhole hanger that Becksvoort uses, center it over the shelf.

Once the four parts have been dry-fitted, I disassemble them and use the tablesaw to chamfer the ends of the uprights and the shelves. When all four parts have been sanded, they can be glued. Since the uprights extend only 2 in. below the lower shelf and the joint is short grain to long grain, I reinforce it with a screw. I drill on a downward angle into the back edge of the upright, drilling through the shelf and into the 2-in. section below.

Drawers seem to float

To add to the airiness of the piece, I chose to suspend the drawers rather than enclose them in a drawer pocket. Both drawers ride on hidden cleats. The cleat for the top drawer has tongues on either end and is glued to the underside of the top shelf. The tongues slide in grooves on the inside face of the drawer

sides near the top. For clearance, the drawer back is not full height. The cleat can be either one solid piece glued with the grain parallel to the shelf, or two narrow pieces screwed to the top, their grain perpendicular to the shelf grain, with allowances for movement. I prefer one solid piece.

The lower drawer's cleat has bevels on its ends instead of tongues. It gets glued to the top of the lower shelf. I glue mating 45° beveled strips to the inside face of the drawer sides just beneath the drawer bottom. The cleat is glued to the bottom shelf with its grain parallel to the shelf.

Hanging it up

Hanging the shelf can be tricky. I use metal keyhole shelf hangers and a method that is almost foolproof. Locate the wall studs and mark them with strips of blue tape. If you

Mortise at the drill press and router. Start at the drill press to establish the radius of the top and bottom of the hanger, then move to a trim router and rout. Blue tape serves as a bright visual guide for routing. Becksvoort uses it as an added precaution to knife lines because the hanger lands so close to the edge. He returns to the drill press to bore holes for the screw heads. Use a chisel to cut the remaining waste to the scribe lines, and then screw the hardware in place.

Two approaches to drawers

The design of this wall shelf is light and airy, so in keeping with that, Becksvoort chose less conventional ways of hanging the drawers. The top drawer runs on a cleat attached to the underside of the top shelf. The bottom drawer engages a beveled cleat beneath it.

Glue in the runners. Rip a 45° angle on two strips of hardwood. Then glue one strip on each side of the drawer. To aid in aligning the runner during glue-up, Becksvoort puts a spacer in the drawer bottom groove. A piece of waxed paper wrapped around the spacer prevents glue from sticking to it. He uses tape as a clamp when gluing the runners in place.

Beveled Runners for the Bottom Drawer

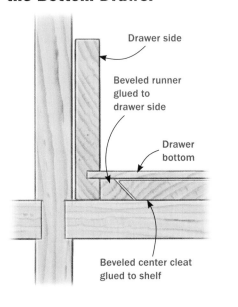

Drawer side

Beveled runner glued to drawer side

Drawer bottom

Beveled center cleat glued to shelf

A cleat guides the drawer. The drawer straddles a solid-wood cleat (above) that's glued to the bottom shelf. Dial in the position of the drawer by clamping the cleat in place from the back (right). Add tape to the upright to create clearance and slide the drawer in place. When the drawer is positioned correctly, mark the placement of the cleat, and then glue and clamp it in place.

The Top Drawer Hangs from a Cleat

Cleat glued to underside of shelf

Drawer side

Rabbet the cleat and groove the drawer sides to match. Create a tongue on the ends of the cleat with a pair of cuts at the tablesaw. Then rip a groove in the drawer sides to fit the cleat.

Flip the shelf upside down to mount the cleat. Clamp the cleat to the underside of the top shelf and slide the drawer in place. When you're happy with the alignment, mark its position and then glue and clamp it in place.

Wipe-on oil and varnish.
The first coat is straight Danish oil. Oil each piece and wipe it off, being careful to remove it all. Let it dry for 48 hours, and then go over all surfaces with 0000 steel wool. The second coat is a mixture of two parts Tried & True varnish oil to one part spar varnish. Wipe thoroughly. After another 48 hours, repeat the varnish coat, and you are finished. Becksvoort uses wax only on the drawer runners.

Tape and dowel centers are key. Set blue tape on the wall where you want the uprights to land. Place dowel centers in the keyhole hanger and use a level to position the shelf on the wall. Press the shelf into the wall. The dowel centers will mark the wall exactly where the screws should go.

won't be hitting studs, using wall anchors instead, place the tape where you want the uprights to go. Please don't just screw into the drywall and call it a day, or the shelf and all your knickknacks will be on the floor at some point. Add a horizontal strip of tape at the height you want your shelf. Insert two ⅜-in. dowel centers into the round portion of the keyhole hangers. With a level on the shelf to make sure it's horizontal, press the shelf against the tape. The points on the dowel centers will leave dimples in the wall. Drill into the dimples and drive the screws, leaving the heads just over ⅛ in. proud of the wall. Hang the shelf on the screws.

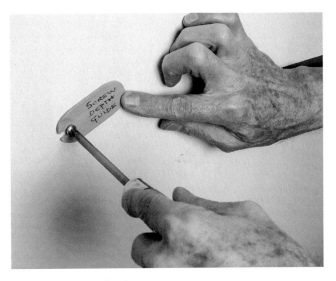

Spacer for screw depth. Becksvoort uses a spacer to know exactly how proud to leave the screw head to work with the keyhole hanger.

Rock your own drawer pulls

River stones serve as drawer pulls. Becksvoort attaches them with a ⅛-in.-dia. shaft made from brass welding rod or machine screws with the heads cut off and secured with 5-min. epoxy. To drill into the stone, clamp it with a plastic clamp and use a cleat to screw the clamp to a board. Use a small squeeze bottle of water to keep the ⅛-in. diamond drill bit cool, catching the water in a shallow pan. Drill slowly and use lots of water. The mortise is ¼ in. to ⅜ in. deep.

A Bevy of Built-Ins

RODNEY DIAZ

A 5-ft.-tall access door off the stair landing, just a couple of steps down from the second floor in our house, makes for an awkward entry to the 13-ft. by 12-ft. space above the kitchen. But once inside, there's a surprisingly large amount of room to move around in under the gable ceiling. Originally an unconditioned storage space, the previous owners attempted to finish out the room with fiberglass-batt insulation behind paneling, padded carpet over a plank subfloor, and rudimentary electrical outlets and a ceiling fixture.

We gutted the room, insulated it properly, and installed outlets and light fixtures to comply with code and coordinate with built-in cabinetry designed to fit the space and maximize the room's functionality. The design of the built-ins was a long time in the making, as it was challenging to figure out how to make the most of this small space. The construction, by comparison, took less time but was no less of an undertaking. The end result is a carefully planned and executed build-out that I hope inspires you to make the most of an underused or overlooked living space in your home or office.

Design notes: A tale of two walls

With a roof pitch of roughly 12-in-12 (give or take a couple of degrees), the steeply sloped ceilings left short kneewalls on either side of the room. At less than 2 ft. tall, this space under the eaves had little practical use. Leaving that floor space open and confining the cabinetry to the gable-end walls creates a sense of a larger space, with a surprisingly roomy 6 ft. between the bed and the desk.

THE WINDOW WALL

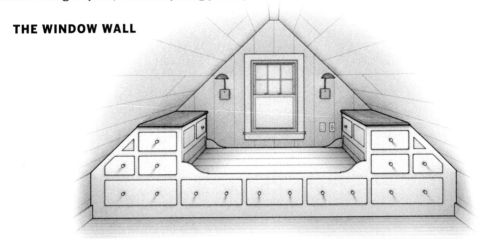

A single double-hung window on the exterior gable wall provides ample natural light, yet limits the options for cabinetry at that end of the room. To maximize storage, a bed platform centered under the window is flanked by matching corner cabinets outfitted with drawers. A trio of drawers under the bed align with the lower drawers in the corner cabinets, tying everything together in a 13-ft.-wide chest of drawers.

THE DOOR WALL

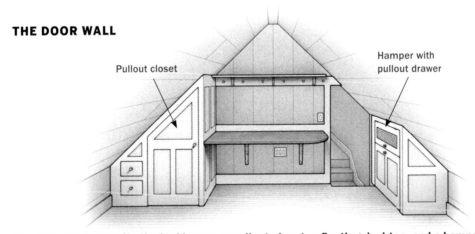

Pullout closet

Hamper with
pullout drawer

The gable wall opposite the bed houses a pullout closet, a floating desktop, and a hamper for dirty clothes. The closet is actually a large pullout drawer mounted on heavy-duty drawer slides, outfitted with a rod for hanging clothes. A pair of drawers fills the void to the left of the closet. The desktop is mounted to the wall with large angle brackets, eliminating desk legs and keeping the floor space open. The corner hamper is tucked under the eave next to the doorway. It has a pullout drawer that holds a laundry basket.

The window wall:
Start with a level base

Building a massive cabinet that spans the width of the room was challenging. Did it make more sense to build the bottom row of large drawers as a unit, then add the smaller drawers on either side of the bed? Or would it be better to build and install the corner cabinets and tie them together with the bed platform? Either way, a level base had to come first, as the floor was out of level by as much as 1½ in., sinking toward the center of the room from the window wall and the eave walls.

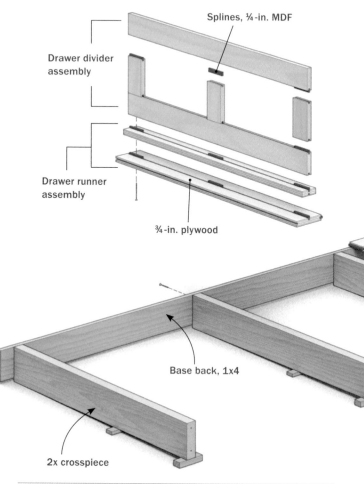

Splines, ¼-in. MDF

Drawer divider assembly

Drawer runner assembly

¾-in. plywood

Base back, 1x4

2x crosspiece

Locate the low spot first. A cutoff from the front of the 1x base is placed at the front center location of the cabinet, also the lowest point in the room. A laser set to the top of the cutoff casts a level line across the wall. At six locations, the height of the level line is measured where 2x framing will run from front to back under the built-ins. Each 2x is ripped to width.

Scribed, shimmed, and screwed. The front of the base is a long 1x6 scribed to the floor. With the back ends of the 2x crosspieces resting on the floor at the wall, the front ends are shimmed flush with the top of the front and screwed together (above). The back ends of the 2x crosspieces are fastened flush with the top of a long 1x4, which is in turn screwed to wall studs (right). With the base secured at the wall, a few angle brackets are screwed to the backside of the base front and fastened to the floor to lock everything in place (far right).

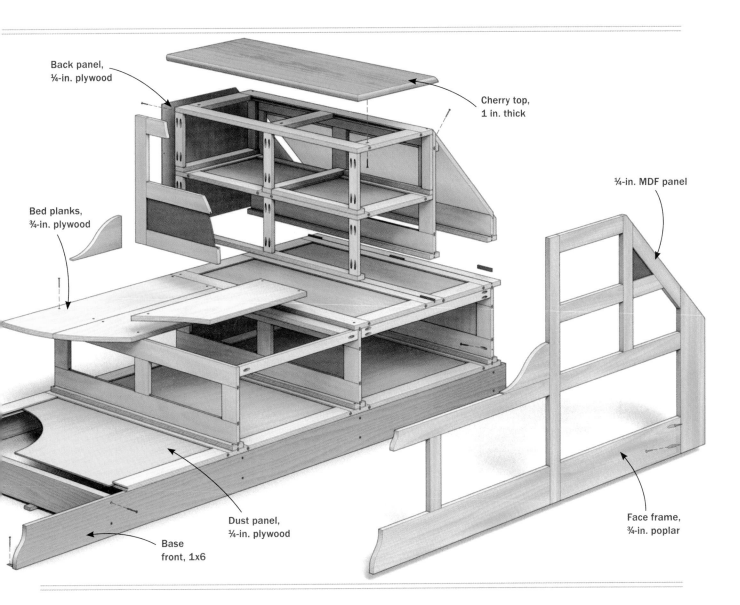

Back panel,
¼-in. plywood

Cherry top,
1 in. thick

¼-in. MDF panel

Bed planks,
¾-in. plywood

Dust panel,
¼-in. plywood

Base
front, 1x6

Face frame,
¾-in. poplar

Lightweight but sturdy framework

The web-frame construction of these chests of drawers was borrowed from traditional furniture making. Using loose-spline joinery makes glue-up easy. The grooves are cut with Freud's box-joint cutter and are exactly ¼ in. wide, which matches the thickness of the MDF splines, resulting in tight glue joints. Where dust panels need to float in the grooves, ¼-in. plywood, which is slightly less thick, slides in easily. This approach also keeps the weight of the carcase down compared to using only ¾-in. plywood.

Groovy joinery. Unless the tablesaw is set up to cut exactly in the center of each workpiece, the potential for misaligned parts during glue-up is high. Make a light pencil mark on one side of each piece and make sure that side is against the fence as it's grooved.

Glue up in stages. The vertical drawer dividers are glued up separately from the flat drawer runners. Once the glue sets, the two are glued and screwed together from the bottom, creating a strong framework to support the bed platform.

Build in layers

Once the cabinet construction began, it became clear that building the corner cabinets separately and connecting them with the bed platform was the way to go. At over 3 ft. square, each cabinet is hefty but slides easily into place thanks to the level base. Cabinet face frames are added to the front and side before installing the bed framework, planks, and face frame.

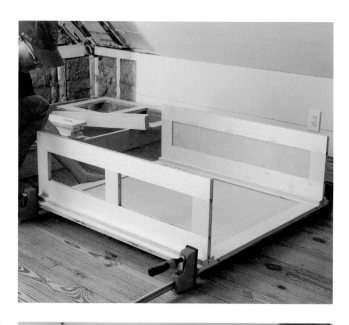

Clamps as a workbench. The bottom web frame is glued up with parallel bar clamps, which proved to be a solid, stable platform for the rest of the cabinet build.

Add the second layer. The upper web frames are added and incorporate a lip to support the ends of the planks that make up the bed platform.

Support where you need it. Blocks clamped to the vertical divider hold the web frame for the top row of drawers at the proper height. Outer supports are pocket-screwed to it and the frame below.

Top off the framework. The subtop is fastened in the same way, while drawer runners for the upper drawers are glued and clamped in place.

Solid backup. The angled subtop is screwed from the outside with angled cleats holding it in position. It and the short outer support are the only solid ¾-in. plywood components.

Slide it into place. With a ¼-in. plywood back added to lock everything square, the assembly comes out of the clamps and slides into final position before being screwed to the base at the outer front edge (right) and the opposite rear corner.

Scribe the face-frame parts. The face frame
is scribed to the ceiling with an angle finder.
The angle is transferred to the miter saw for a
matching cut.

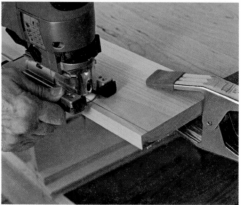

Scribe, scribe again. Scribed to the wall with
a compass and to the floor with a scrap of new
flooring, the side and bottom edges are trimmed
with a jigsaw.

Assemble the face frame. The parts scribed to the wall and the floor are pocket-screwed together. The assembly is then clamped in place while subsequent parts are cut and fit one at a time. The last piece of the puzzle is a triangular ¼-in. MDF panel set into grooves cut in the same fashion as the web-frame joinery.

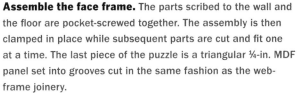

A clean front. The assembled face frame is clamped in position and screwed from behind, leaving a clean front that needs no nail holes filled. The end panel facing the bed is installed using the same technique.

Fill in the gap. With the plywood bed planks installed, cleats are installed between drawer dividers to add rigidity behind the face frame at the front edge of the bed.

Cut curves in place. Rectangular stock for the curved bed-rail brackets is easier to attach to the face frame before shaping with a jigsaw and sandpaper.

Pulling it all together. Like the corner cabinets, the bed's face frame is installed as a unit, pocket-screwed from behind, except for the bottom, which had to be face-nailed.

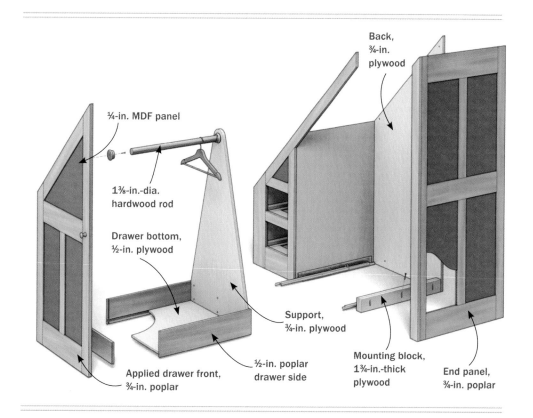

Back, ¾-in. plywood

¼-in. MDF panel

1⅜-in.-dia. hardwood rod

Drawer bottom, ½-in. plywood

Support, ¾-in. plywood

½-in. poplar drawer side

Mounting block, 1¾-in.-thick plywood

End panel, ¾-in. poplar

Applied drawer front, ¾-in. poplar

The door wall: A pair of pullout boxes

The closet and the hamper function in a similar fashion, with drawer boxes riding on full-extension drawer slides. The closet is outfitted with a false front door and a rear upright panel supporting a closet rod. The hamper works in the same way, with a cabinet-door panel on the front of a box that holds a laundry basket.

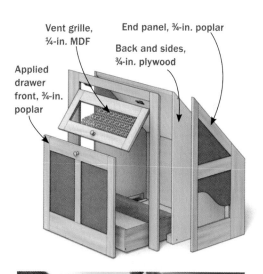

Vent grille, ¼-in. MDF

End panel, ¾-in. poplar

Back and sides, ¾-in. plywood

Applied drawer front, ¾-in. poplar

Get the funk out. The hamper is a miniature version of the closet in both form and function. Its one unique feature is a laser-cut ¼-in. MDF vent grille in the hinged hanging door for airing out dirty laundry.

Square the opening. A plywood mounting block is squared flush with the front of the corner cabinet and pocket-screwed to the floor.

Install the end panel. The end panel is pocket-screwed from behind to the mounting block at the bottom and to a ¾-in. plywood back panel that's secured to the wall.

Hidden hardware. Blum undermount drawer slides enable the closet to smoothly open and close while supporting a rack of hanging clothes.

Mark in place. The face frame is assembled with the top diagonal piece left long. Once clamped in place, the horn is marked where it meets the end panel and trimmed to fit.

Nail it off. A plywood cleat fastened to the ceiling provides backing for nailing the top edge of the face frame and the end panel.

A floating desktop

A 5-ft.-long panel of solid cherry is fastened to wall-mounted workstation brackets. Absent legs or an apron, the surface appears to float against the wall. Above the desktop is a shelf mounted on top of a Shaker-style peg rail.

A touch of Shaker trim. A 10-in.-deep shelf is pocket-screwed from behind to the peg board before the assembly is nailed to wall studs.

Bracketology. Aluminum brackets from A&M Hardware are screwed to wall studs. Weighing only 4 lb. each, the two brackets support over 1400 lb. together under load testing.

Turn the corner. The corner of the desk is curved with a 13-in. radius to ease entry into the room. The edge is softened with a bullnose profile routed with a ⅜-in.-radius roundover bit.

Cabinet tops and drawers

The corner cabinets are capped with 1-in.-thick solid cherry tops that mirror the desktop. Unlike the closet and hamper, the drawers slide on drawer runners built into the cabinets.

A consistent overhang. Each cabinet top is scribed to the wall, then an angled cut on the back pins it under the ceiling. The tops are marked from underneath where they meet the face frames. Then the top is flipped upside down and a 1-in. offset is marked and cut.

The movement you need. The leading edge of the top is held in place by screws fastened from below through slotted holes in the subtop, allowing for seasonal movement. The exposed edges are shaped with the same bullnose profile found on the desk.

Easy sliders. A coat of paste wax applied to the drawer runners in the cabinets and to the bottoms of the drawer sides make even the biggest drawers slide in and out with ease.

Built-Ins for Odd Spaces

GARY STRIEGLER

J ust about every job I work on has one or two odd cabinets that aren't quite what your typical kitchen-and-bath cabinet shop is used to dealing with. What I call "off-angle cabinets" are a great example. Sometimes you find them tucked under a stairway, but they are also common in second stories with sloping ceilings. The room shown here was an unfinished bonus room that the owners wanted to turn into a play and study room for two young boys, and I had to make two off-angle cabinets to fit against the slope of the gable roof.

I developed a method to build these odd-shaped cabinets so they fit every time. It all starts with the back; I scribe-fit a piece of ¼-in. plywood that will become the cabinet back, but first I use it as a template to build the cabinet. The face frame exactly matches the template, but the cabinet box doesn't. Instead, when I draw the layout on the template, I shift the lines for the sides close to the wall and ceiling in about ¼ in. That leaves ¼ in. of face frame overhanging the cabinet box to be scribed to fit the wall and ceiling.

My construction methods for off-angle cabinets are a little bit different than standard cabinets. I essentially build a box within a box. The interior box supports the shelves and reinforces all the joints in the outside box. For the room here, I realized it would be a lot easier to get all the pieces of material I needed up the narrow stairway than to bring the assembled cabinet upstairs. So I started by ripping ¾-in. plywood into eight 11¼-in. strips in my shop. I also cut and sized all the lumber I needed to make the face frames. I planned to make all the plywood cuts with a track saw, but first I had to figure out what angle to cut the plywood. I cut a scrap of lumber and made a couple of test cuts comparing them to the layout on the plywood back; it turned out to be 44°.

I'm sure there are some carpenters who could just take some measurements and go build this cabinet. When possible, I am much more comfortable marking the length in place than measuring. Working from a full-scale pattern reduces the chance of error, in my experience; once I have the pattern right, I just cut pieces to match and put them together. It is pretty simple, but I'll take simple every chance I get.

Mark the perimeter. Measure off the floor to mark the top and bottom of the cabinet back, and off the wall to mark its width, then use a level to extend the marks level and plumb.

Rough the back. Measure the lengths on the wall, transfer them to the plywood back, then use a track saw to cut the plywood to its rough shape.

Scribe to fit. Hold the plywood back in position on the level lines and check the fit. If there are any gaps along the wall or sloped ceiling, mark and scribe it to fit.

Mark offsets. I draw lines 1 in. in from the edge of the sides that butt into the wall and ceiling, which leaves the plywood back hanging over ¼ in. A 3-in. offset at the bottom accommodates the bottom shelf and a hardwood cleat for fastening to the wall. Use an angle finder or make test cuts to determine the cut angle for the intersecting wall and ceiling planes, which is needed later.

Make a template

It all starts with the back panel, which also serves as a template for the carcase. I already know the height and width I'm aiming for, and how far off the floor it has to be to accommodate a built-in-desk below. I simply draw the outline of the cabinet's perimeter on the wall, then cut and scribe the back to fit in that space.

Build the box

I prefer to mark trim lengths in place rather than use a tape, and I use that same method for the parts of these cabinets. The layout lines and the edge of the plywood back are my starting points. I precut all of the plywood to width on a tablesaw at my shop, and cut all the parts to length on-site with a track saw.

Mark in place. When possible, use the layout lines as a guide to mark where to cut pieces to length.

Fasten as you go. Fasten parts as they're cut for a tight fit, for accurate marks, and to ensure nothing gets mixed up.

Prep the pockets. Pocket-hole screws secure the face frame along the sides that butt into the wall and ceiling. Drill the pocket holes before the entire perimeter of the cabinet is fastened to make things easier.

Space it out. Adjustable shelves don't work with this cabinet, so I space them evenly with pieces of plywood cut to the height between shelves, and nail them to the sides of the box with 1¼-in. brads.

Hide the fasteners. Fasten the shelves through their tops down into their supporting spacers using 2-in. brads. The next layer of spacers will conceal these nails—just one less thing to fill before finishing.

Find the intersection. To determine where the spacer goes on the angled side, I simply pull a tape square off the previous shelf and mark where the shelf's height intersects the slope.

Two-part spacer. Depending on your shelf layout, the spacer on the sloped side may require two pieces. The cut angle identified earlier (in this case, 44°) comes into play here.

Slide carefully. Go slow when adding shelves in the upper sloped portion to avoid damaging the sharp edges created by the angled cut.

Stiffen and trim

The plywood back and 1-in. (nominal) face frame give the cabinet rigidity, and cleats provide the needed strength to hold it on the wall. Trim is optional, but I never miss an opportunity to add a little flourish.

Back it up. Align the back flush with the side that will be visible in the room, leaving the edge against the wall running long. This excess gets trimmed later.

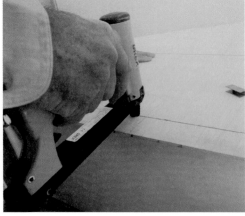

Staple liberally. Because this construction method is a little unorthodox, I fasten the back with ⅝-in.-long ⅜-in.-dia. crown staples around the entire perimeter and into the shelves roughly 3 in. on center to add rigidity and holding power.

Assemble the face frames. I build the face frames using the back template as a guide. Because the back is slightly larger than the cabinet box, the face frame will overhang slightly, to be scribed to the wall and ceiling if necessary.

Fasten the face. Glue around the entire front edge of the box, then clamp the face frame to the box along the bottom and side that faces into the room, and fasten the hidden sides, which overhang the box, with pocket screws. Allow the glue to set before removing the clamps and sanding.

Cleat it. Add 2¼-in. cleats to the bottom and upper interior of the box for attachment. Cut the pieces for a tight fit, then fasten with 2-in. brads through the sides and crown staples through the back.

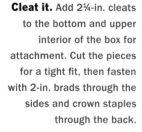
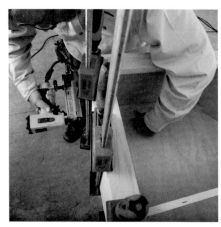

Add the nosing. To hide the edges of the plywood shelves, cut and fasten molding with glue and 2-in. brads.

Plane it flush. Trim the bit of the back that overhangs the cabinet before testing its fit against the wall and ceiling. Scribe the face frame as necessary for a tight fit, then fasten the cabinet to the studs with long screws through the top and bottom cleats.

Trim it out. Though not entirely necessary, I like to add a little trim to these odd cabinets. The top has a routed-edge top cap over a piece of panel mold. A narrow scribe mold covers the plywood back.

Build a Desk Bed

NATHAN RINNE

Hiding in Plain Sight

A counterbalanced lift mechanism, rotating desk hardware, and folding steel legs allow the desk to convert to a bed in seconds. The desk, which can hold up to 45 lb., stays parallel to the floor as the bed is lowered, so you can leave everything on it.

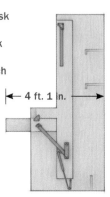

4 ft. 1 in.

7 ft. 1 in.

3 ft. 1¼ in.

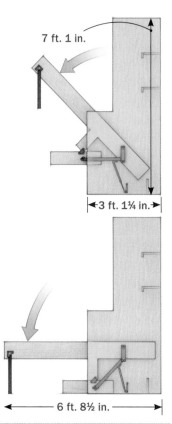

6 ft. 8½ in.

The home office has always seemed like a luxury to me. Unwilling to give up a spare bedroom, I've settled for a small desk in a corner of my living room for years. I'm sure this is a dilemma for many people. The first time I saw a desk bed by Hiddenbed USA, I was blown away. It's similar to the Murphy-bed concept, but in addition to the foldaway bed,

Double Duty

Steel hinges, legs, and desk pivots made by Hiddenbed USA are the secret to the desk-to-bed transformation. Hardware, direct from the manufacturer and from several online sources, is available for twin and double beds in both vertical and horizontal arrangements, and for queen beds in vertical only. You can cut the plywood parts yourself using provided shop drawings, or you can buy them precut in several wood species from the hardware manufacturer. You can also have the parts cut at a local cabinet shop with CNC toolpath files provided by the hardware manufacturer.

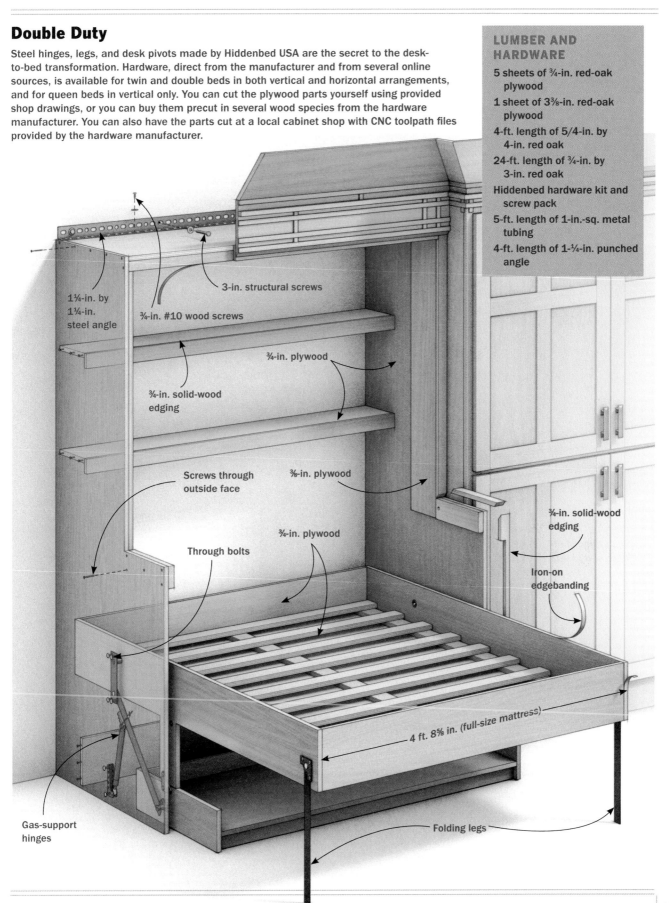

LUMBER AND HARDWARE

5 sheets of ¾-in. red-oak plywood

1 sheet of 3⅜-in. red-oak plywood

4-ft. length of 5/4-in. by 4-in. red oak

24-ft. length of ¾-in. by 3-in. red oak

Hiddenbed hardware kit and screw pack

5-ft. length of 1-in.-sq. metal tubing

4-ft. length of 1-¼-in. punched angle

1¼-in. by 1¼-in. steel angle

¾-in. #10 wood screws

3-in. structural screws

¾-in. solid-wood edging

¾-in. plywood

⅜-in. plywood

Screws through outside face

Through bolts

¾-in. plywood

¾-in. solid-wood edging

Iron-on edgebanding

Gas-support hinges

4 ft. 8⅝ in. (full-size mattress)

Folding legs

Cut and prep the parts. The casework is made from ¾-in. plywood with appearance-grade veneers on both sides. Exposed edges are covered with solid stock or edgebanding. Prepping the parts is labor intensive. The 31-page collection of shop drawings included with the hardware kit shows how to cut and drill every part for the bed, desk, and case. The measurements are metric and must be followed precisely or the bed won't open and close correctly.

Make space. Cutting the plywood and handling the uncut sheets is physically taxing and takes up a surprising amount of room. An empty one-car garage is about the smallest space that will accommodate the cutting and assembly of a double- or queen-size desk bed.

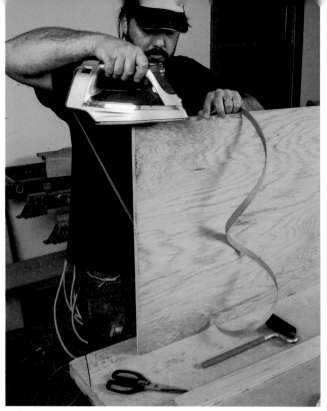

Band the edges. You can conceal plywood edges with solid stock, or you can use edgebanding tape with hot-melt glue on the back. The glue is heated with a clothes iron, and then the edgeband is rolled with a laminate roller.

It turned out to be a fun, if slightly grueling, undertaking. As with every new project in the carpentry business, I learned a lot, including how I would do some things differently the next time around. Here are some of the lessons I learned.

Multiple kit options

These beds come in vertical and horizontal configurations in twin, double, and queen sizes. My clients wanted closets on both sides of the bed, but I had only a 13-ft. wall to work with. They opted for a vertical full bed (4 ft. 5 in. wide), which is the smallest size that will sleep two people. This decision is important not just for overall design but also because the gas pistons that lift and lower the bed are matched to the anticipated size and weight of the mattress. Although you can order these beds as kits with the plywood parts already cut, I decided to cut the parts

there is an attached desk. Not only that, but the desk remains parallel to the floor as the bed is opened and closed, so you can leave everything on it.

After viewing a web video of a desk bed, I knew I had to build one. I pitched the idea to prospective clients for years before I finally got a call from a couple looking for a conventional hidden bed with closets on both sides. After I offered them a ridiculously good deal, they agreed to incorporate the desk into the design, and I had my chance to give this project a go.

Build the desk. The desk, which is almost 5 ft. wide, requires a piece of steel tubing to prevent it from sagging. The 1-in.-sq. tube is cut to length, drilled, and then fastened with 1½-in. screws to the underside of the plywood desktop.

apron hides the desk's steel reinforcement. It's fastened to the bottom of the desktop with screws in closely spaced pocket holes drilled using a pocket-hole jig.

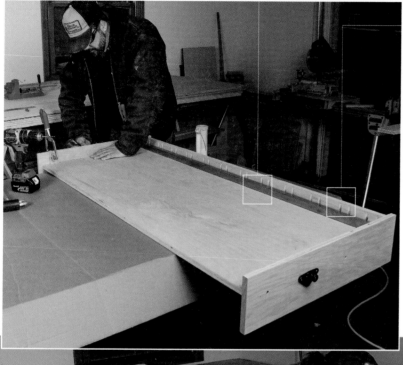

Swiveling desk sides. The sides of the desk are edgebanded and screwed to the desktop. Pivots, included in the hardware kit, are secured through the sides into the top with screws and through bolts. A clamp and a wood spacer ensure that the sides overhang the top evenly.

Strong, swiveling connection. Color-matched machine screws and matching T-nuts fasten the desktop's top pivot in place. The through-bolted connection allows the desk to remain parallel to the floor as the bed is raised and lowered, and it can support up to 45 lb. on the desktop.

myself so that I could scribe the casework to better fit the bowed wall on which it was being built.

I ordered the hardware kit and bought the oak plywood and 1x face-frame stock from a local supplier. Somehow during the hardware ordering process I was never told that there's also a kit with all of the nuts, bolts, screws, and fasteners to assemble the bed and the desk. Fortunately, my local home center had most of what I needed and substitutes for the rest, but it was an unanticipated hassle. (My advice: make sure to specify both kits when you place an order.)

All the small details, all the big parts

Building the bed using the 31-page instruction manual was challenging. For example, the dimensions are metric, and converting those dimensions to fractions leaves you with numbers that are too fine to use easily. (Ever mark ¹⁄₆₄ of an inch?) For someone like me who has never thought outside of the imperial-system box, this took some getting used to. My solution was to run out and buy a metric tape measure.

I should also mention that there are nearly four dozen pieces to cut and a substantial amount of holes to drill in precise locations. If you are not proficient at reading diagrams or are just looking to save time, you can get the plywood parts precut from Hiddenbed USA. You can also get toolpath files from the company and have the parts cut locally by a CNC shop, which is what I would do in the future.

Having the parts cut by a CNC shop has advantages when space is a concern, because

Build the bed. The double- and queen-size versions of a desk bed are wider than a single sheet of plywood. A seam in the center of the panel looks better than if it were offset. The two roughly 2-ft. 4-in. panels are joined in the center with wood glue and biscuits, and the seam is hidden with ¼-in.-thick flat stock.

Site-built bed springs. Slats made from 4¾-in.-wide pieces of plywood consume the offcuts from larger pieces, support the mattress, and allow air circulation underneath. The completed bed box is unwieldy and weighs 120 lb., so you'll need help getting it to its final location.

cutting and organizing the parts for these huge boxes takes a lot of time and space. Also worth noting is that the cabinet that holds the bed is too big to fit through a 36-in. door and must be assembled in the room where it will reside.

Although the parts are big, the joinery is straightforward. The plans call for Confirmat screws to assemble the cases, but I used high-quality construction screws and wood glue. I concealed the screws on the bed cabinet with the 24-in.-deep wardrobe cabinets on both sides of the bed cabinet.

Once the bed cabinet is assembled and in place, you have to attach the bed frame. It's heavy and awkward, so you will definitely need a helper. You also have to create a sturdy cabinet-to-wall connection so that the massive bed box won't tip as the bed is raised and lowered. I used a 4-ft. piece of punched steel angle (like what you would use to hang a garage door) that I screwed to the top of the bed cabinet and into the studs with structural screws.

Making a massive box look good

After the cases for this project were in place, it became obvious that the panel concealing the bottom of the bed was simply too plain. Taking cues from the homeowners' Craftsman-style decorating, I decided to add some applied wood strips. Using ¼-in.-thick solid oak, I tested the layout of the applied molding until I thought it looked right.

One good thing about the expansive bed cabinet is that you have a good amount of space to create on. My advice is to step back and look while experimenting until the arrangement looks right to you.

Assemble in place. The case for the bed is too large to fit through a 36-in. door, so you'll need to assemble it in the space where it will reside. Once the parts are screwed together, the case is plumbed and fastened to the floor and wall framing with structural screws.

Double drilling. The hinge and lift mechanisms require identical holes for through bolts on both sides of the cabinets. It's faster and more accurate to drill both sides at once. Triple-check their locations so that the mechanisms work correctly when the desk bed is complete.

Mount the hardware. The hinges and lift supports are bolted to the bed cabinet's sides using locking nuts and through bolts. Gas pistons help balance the weight of the bed box and the mattress. The pistons are matched to the bed size.

Connect the bed to its cabinet. The bed box is connected to the hinges with large-shouldered through bolts (included with the kit) that are tightened with a 10-mm hex wrench. Most hex-key assortments don't include a wrench that big, but you can find them at auto-parts stores.

Install the locks. A pair of sliding pins keep the bed in the upright position, even when the desk is fully loaded. The pins attach to the desk assembly with three screws and line up with matching holes that are drilled into the bed case.

Cover the edges. Exposed edges on the case are covered with 1¼-in.-wide solid stock, which also hides the gap between the folding bed box and the bed cabinet. The stock is fastened with 18-ga. brads and wood glue. Miters hide the stock's end grain.

Spaces within Spaces

MARK HUTKER

The houses we build are meant for family gathering. Increasingly, that means creating hybrid spaces that can accommodate large groups when the whole family is present but that also feel comfortable for just Mom and Dad. The key is to create spaces within spaces—nooks and recesses with their own unique attributes that create intimacy in bigger rooms.

Inhabiting these spaces can be very pleasing. Being half in and half out of a public space fosters the feeling of being connected to people and activities while experiencing the shelter, relative privacy, or utility of a smaller, customized haven. We often make desirable berths out of edges and corners of rooms that might otherwise be underused, turning them into breakfast spots, window seats, and even playful hideouts for children. Purposeful lighting, custom cushions, and built-in storage bays are little luxuries that enhance the specific identities of these alcoves.

4 design touchstones

To inform the design of spaces within spaces, focus on four main aspects:

SCALABILITY
Can a large room have one or more smaller, ancillary spaces that function with the whole as well as independently?

ADJACENCY
Do the rooms relate to one another in ways that make sense for a variety of inhabitants and activities?

MATERIAL AND THEMATIC CONNECTION
How will the smaller spaces relate to the larger ones?

RIGHT-SIZING
Does the room's size foster the kinds of activities it is designed for?

Great-room island

The clients who commissioned this great room wanted a space that would be comfortable for both large family gatherings and intimate weekends. Vaulted ceilings and two stories of windows bring light and openness to the living room, making it a dynamic space for entertaining. A lower, wood-paneled ceiling gives the dining area a more intimate atmosphere for meals. The built-in bench nestled between the living and dining areas takes this intimacy to an even smaller scale, providing a harbor that's perfect for a nap or additional living-room seating when needed. Clear wood trim helps to link all three spaces.

Living

Built-in bench

Dining

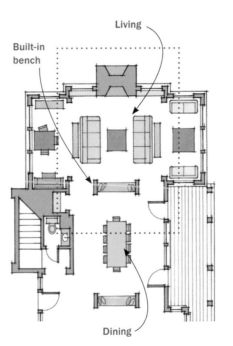

Cooking and eating

Working kitchen

Breakfast nook

This farmhouse kitchen is broken into several different spaces that are thematically linked by shapes yet separated by material choices. Two large islands and a niche for the custom range create distinct, rectangular work zones. To create a visual link between these zones, the same stone is used for their counters. A rectangular, weathered-wood dining table breaks materially from the other zones, suggesting a shift in purpose: from the work of preparing meals to relaxing and eating. Scaled for conversation and comfort, the table and a custom bench occupy a nook that is surrounded on three sides by windows. Timber framing traverses the entire kitchen ceiling, in simple spans across the working areas and in a more elaborate pattern above the dining nook.

Hearth and bar

The focal point of this home's great room is a central fireplace that allows circular movement between the great room and the kitchen and dining areas. A wet bar hidden behind the fireplace creates a sheltered eddy for private conversations. Fostering this sense of shelter at the wet bar is a low pergola that contrasts with the high, timber-trussed ceilings of the overall space. Exposed stonework connects this interstitial space to the great room, while its cabinetry links it to the kitchen beyond.

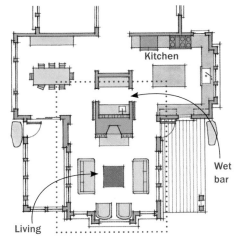

Kitchen

Wet bar

Living

Custom Cabinets: An Inside Look

BRENT BENNER

Designers normally don't provide construction details beyond elevation drawings for kitchen cabinets. As a cabinet builder, it's my job to fill in the details. Regardless of style, the cabinet boxes, or carcases, are similar. The differences in how I build each style of cabinet lie in how the doors and drawers relate to the frames. Euro-style cabinets have no face frames; the doors and drawers cover the carcase edges. Overlay and inset cabinets have traditional face frames, but the former's doors and drawers overlay the cabinet faces, while the latter's are inset within the faces.

All Cabinets Start With a Basic Carcase

All styles of cabinets have carcases made of similar materials and joinery. The base cabinet carcases are sized to sit on a 4-in.-high base, usually made from plywood scrap and recessed from the front of the cabinets to create a toe space. This frame is leveled so the cabinet carcases can be placed on it without having to fuss with each one. I use prefinished maple plywood for all carcase parts. For cabinets wider than 3 ft., a row of holes for shelf pins is drilled down the center of the back. Heavier-duty shelves get a ¾-in. by 1½-in. hardwood strip set in a dado along the back edge for additional support.

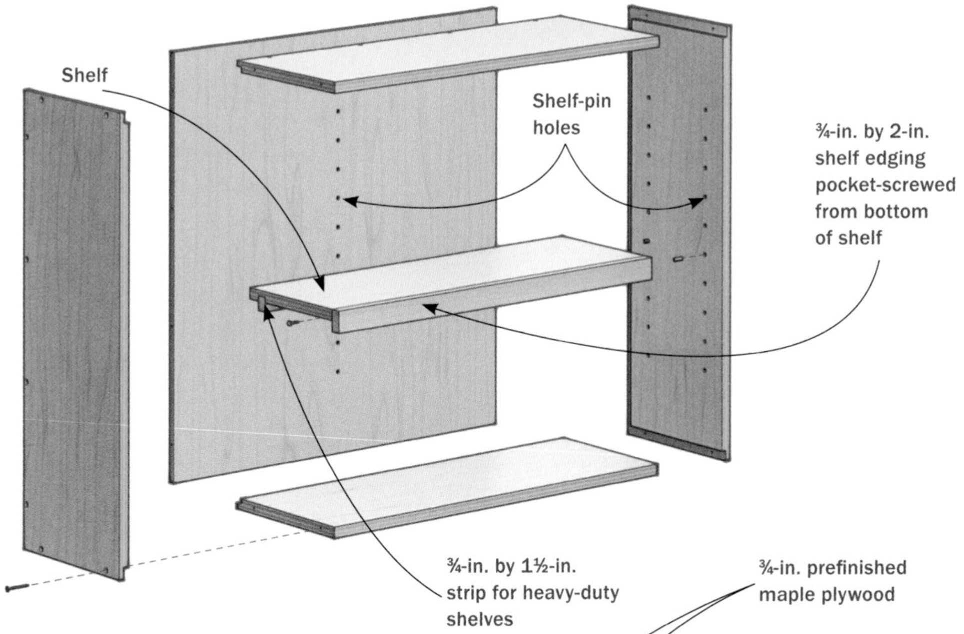

Shelf

Shelf-pin holes

¾-in. by 2-in. shelf edging pocket-screwed from bottom of shelf

¾-in. by 1½-in. strip for heavy-duty shelves

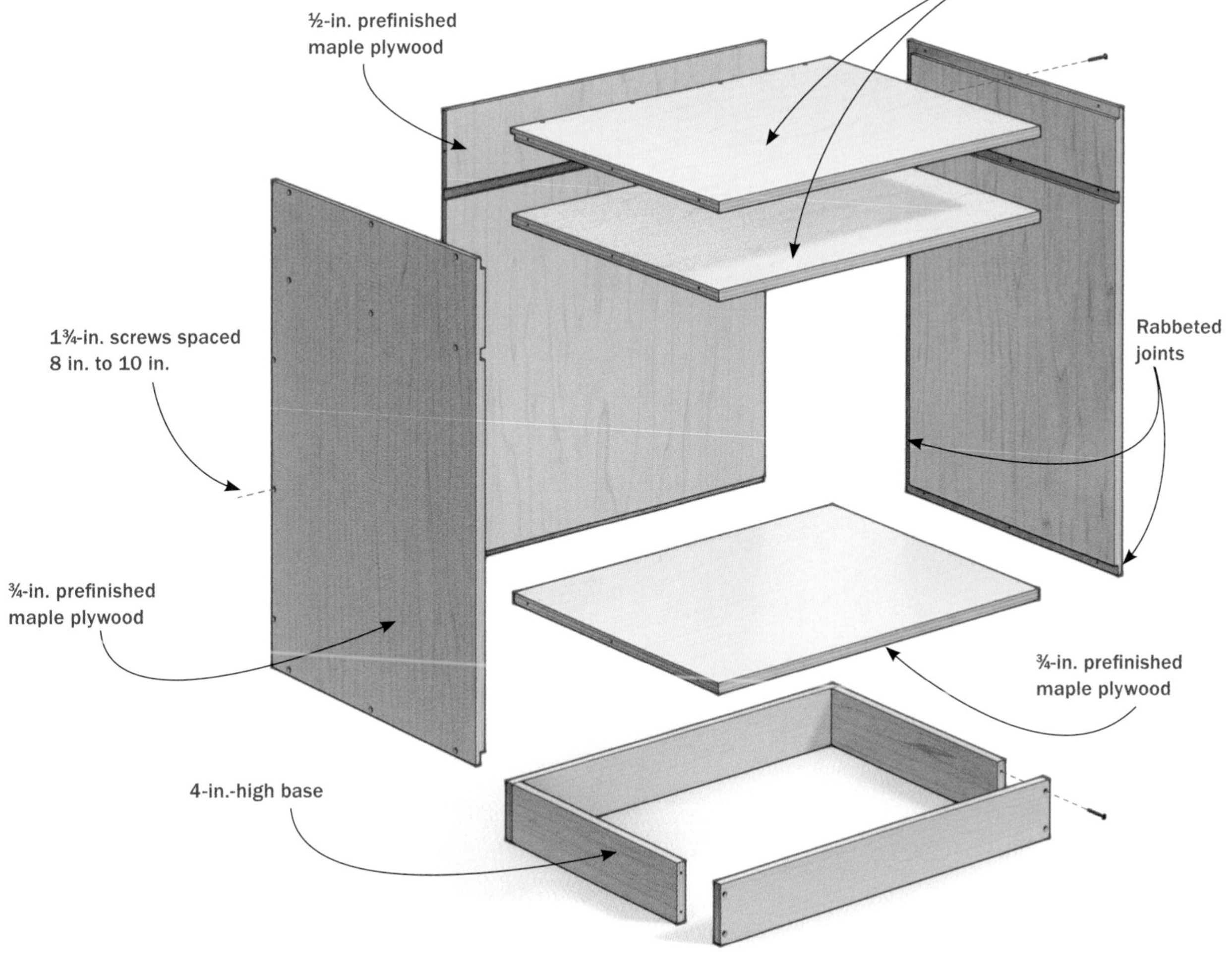

¾-in. prefinished maple plywood

½-in. prefinished maple plywood

1¾-in. screws spaced 8 in. to 10 in.

Rabbeted joints

¾-in. prefinished maple plywood

¾-in. prefinished maple plywood

4-in.-high base

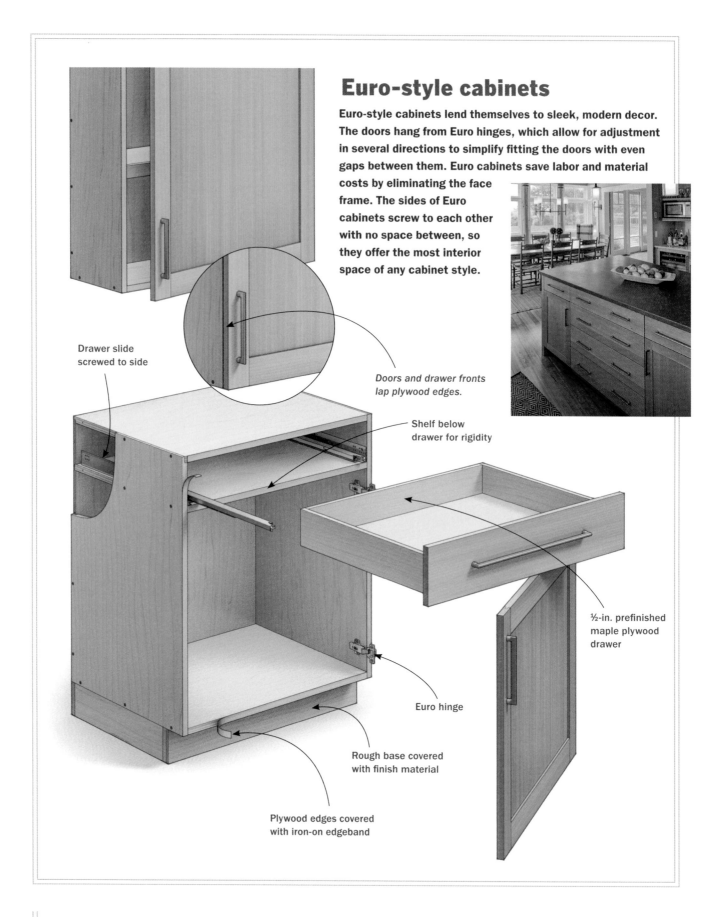

Euro-style cabinets

Euro-style cabinets lend themselves to sleek, modern decor. The doors hang from Euro hinges, which allow for adjustment in several directions to simplify fitting the doors with even gaps between them. Euro cabinets save labor and material costs by eliminating the face frame. The sides of Euro cabinets screw to each other with no space between, so they offer the most interior space of any cabinet style.

Drawer slide screwed to side

Doors and drawer fronts lap plywood edges.

Shelf below drawer for rigidity

½-in. prefinished maple plywood drawer

Euro hinge

Rough base covered with finish material

Plywood edges covered with iron-on edgeband

Overlay cabinets

For a traditional look, overlay cabinets have a face frame made from ¾-in. by 2¼-in. hardwood, joined together and to the carcase with pocket screws. The larger space between doors and drawers makes adjusting them easier than with Euro cabinets. The face frame overhangs the outside and inside of the carcase. This limits access to the interior, and, compared to Euro cabinets, the drawers and interior space will be smaller.

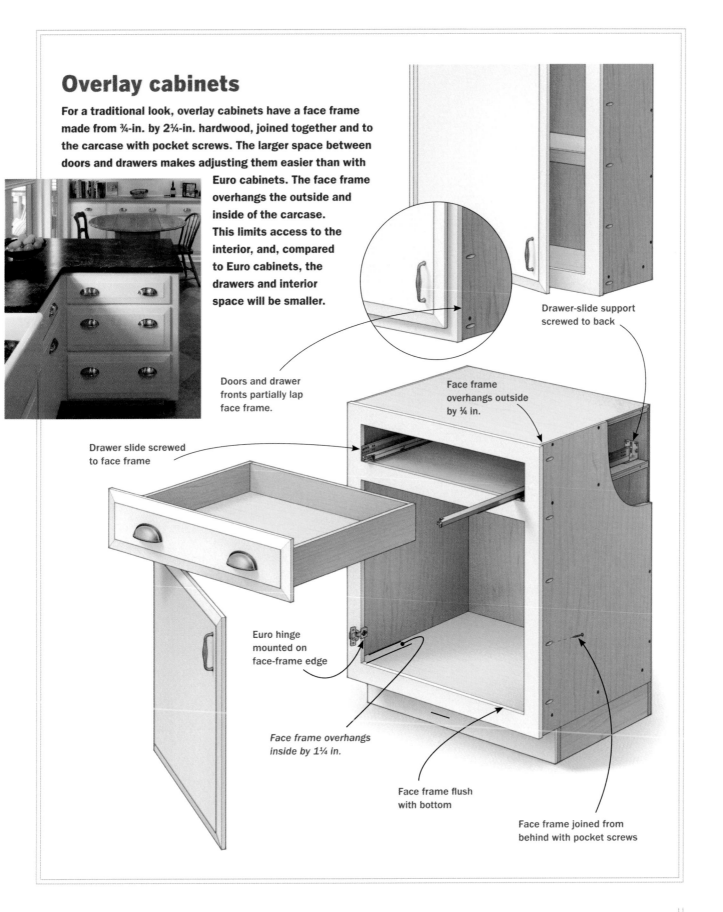

Doors and drawer fronts partially lap face frame.

Drawer-slide support screwed to back

Face frame overhangs outside by ¼ in.

Drawer slide screwed to face frame

Euro hinge mounted on face-frame edge

Face frame overhangs inside by 1¼ in.

Face frame flush with bottom

Face frame joined from behind with pocket screws

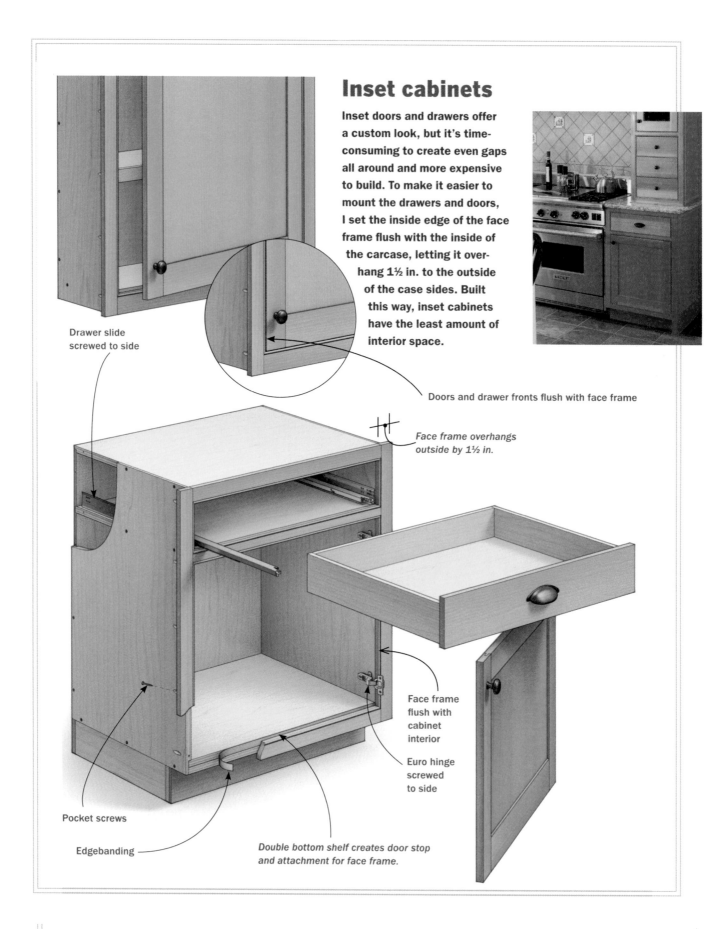

Inset cabinets

Inset doors and drawers offer a custom look, but it's time-consuming to create even gaps all around and more expensive to build. To make it easier to mount the drawers and doors, I set the inside edge of the face frame flush with the inside of the carcase, letting it overhang 1½ in. to the outside of the case sides. Built this way, inset cabinets have the least amount of interior space.

Drawer slide screwed to side

Doors and drawer fronts flush with face frame

Face frame overhangs outside by 1½ in.

Face frame flush with cabinet interior

Euro hinge screwed to side

Pocket screws

Edgebanding

Double bottom shelf creates door stop and attachment for face frame.

Installing Frameless Cabinets

AARON BUTT

I put in my first set of kitchen cabinets more than 15 years ago, and I've done dozens of installations since. All of these cabinets have fallen into one of two categories: face frame, which is what most American cabinet manufacturers produce, and frameless, which was first popularized in Europe. Face-frame cabinets are just what they sound like: They have a frame that attaches to the front of the cabinet boxes to keep them square and to mount doors. The frames typically extend beyond the sides of the actual cabinet box, so it's easy to trim or plane them to correct for extra-tight or out-of-plumb conditions. You can also extend the frame or use fillers to close gaps between cabinets, walls, and appliances. These are luxuries you do not have with frameless cabinets.

Frameless boxes fit together tightly, and the reveals between their full-overlay doors and drawers are small and uniform, so any problems are especially obvious. A ¼-in. difference between the design and field conditions can mean time-consuming and complicated workarounds. The upsides of these cabinets are that they're easier to reach into and they're more spacious than face-frame cabinets.

To prevent problems, I like to field-verify all the measurements and compare them to the shop drawings before the cabinets are built. When we field-verify, we also check for out-of-plumb and out-of-level conditions.

Find the high spot. We start by projecting a level laser line onto the wall. The laser line's height doesn't matter; its only purpose is to act as a reference, allowing us to measure down to the floor in several places on every wall to find the highest spot. Then, we measure up from the high spot and mark the wall at 34¾ in.—the standard 36-in. cabinet height minus the thickness of a typical 1¼-in. countertop—and use a long level or chalklines to continue this level line on every wall that will receive cabinets.

Locate the boxes. With the control line established, we refer to the plans and mark the width and edges of each individual cabinet—uppers, lowers, and all appliance locations—to verify that the cabinet plans and the actual room are in agreement.

This chapter follows one of our typical custom frameless cabinet installations. The kitchen isn't especially big, but it has all of the elements common to this room: upper and lower cabinets, an island, and special enclosures for some large appliances. Installing custom frameless cabinets takes longer than off-the-shelf framed cabinets—this kitchen took two skilled carpenters and a helper a full work week to install 16 cabinets and build the island. But I enjoy the challenge of installing kitchen cabinets because it uses such a wide set of skills. The work requires thought and meticulousness, and you can enjoy a real sense of accomplishment when the job is done.

Layout is everything

We do a comprehensive layout of the cabinets before putting anything in place. It's the first step to ensuring the uppers and lowers are in the right spot and that they're plumb, level, and square, even if the walls are not. We snap level control lines and write individual box dimensions on the walls. This step also verifies that the design and field conditions are in sync.

Installing uppers

I prefer to install upper cabinets first, because it's easier to lift them into position and fasten them without the lowers in the way. We usually start installing cabinets in the middle of a wall, so two of us can work at the same time on opposite sides of a center cabinet. In this case, the sink wall had a bank of windows and the uppers

Label everything. Next, we mark each cabinet along with its corresponding position on the wall. Then, we remove all drawers, doors, and shelving from the cabinets, labeling each part. We set aside everything but the boxes, ideally in another room so it won't be damaged.

Ledger makes upper cabinets level. Fastening a 2x board along the layout line with 3-in. screws into the framing ensures wall cabinets are installed level and at the right elevation. It also helps hold the cabinets while they are fastened to the wall. The screw holes will be hidden by a tile backsplash or filled and sanded by the painter.

Screw into solid backing. When we can, we install blocking between studs for every cabinet, ensuring every box is secure and that screws can be arranged in a consistent manner. Without blocking, we locate every stud and arrange screws as consistently as possible.

Spacers in corners. A spacer at blind corners allows doors to open without hitting each other. We find that it's easier to attach it at the correct reveal before lifting the box.

Room for adjustment. Spacing blind-corner cabinets slightly away from neighboring walls compensates for out-of-plumb and out-of-square conditions. Frameless cabinets can be forced out of square if they're pushed tight to an out-of-plumb wall. We make sure the box is tight to the ledger and the sides are plumb before fastening.

Ducts and wires in range hoods. After finding the center of roughed-in ducts, pipes, and wires, we transfer the measurements to the box. We mark large holes with a compass and cut them with a jigsaw when a hole saw is too small.

Holes for wires. A ¾-in. spade bit is ideal for boring small holes for wires, but we always drill from both sides to avoid chipping the veneer. For large holes, we use a jigsaw and veneer blade, such as Starrett's Dual Cut.

Fish and lift. After test-fitting the range hood in its cabinet and making the holes for the duct and wires, we fish the cables and ducts through the cabinet as we lift it into place, then fasten it to the wall.

Water and waste in sink base. We strike level and plumb lines around plumbing rough-ins to establish their center points. Then we measure between the lines for the box layout and plumbing rough-ins and transfer those measurements to the cabinets. Making cutouts with a hole saw from both sides avoids tearout. When finished, we set the cabinet in place to check the fit.

Join boxes. After the first lower cabinet is in place, each individual cabinet is then set, shimmed level and plumb, and clamped and screwed to the adjoining cabinets.

flanked the opening, so we each took a side of the window opening to work on. Some carpenters screw a bunch of boxes together and install them as a unit. We do that sometimes, but when we split sides, it's easier to go one at a time so we don't have to struggle lifting the boxes, which might lead to accidental damage.

Installing lowers

In old houses, we install frameless cabinets one at a time—without a face frame, you can easily distort the box if you're handling or shimming more than one simultaneously. Before fastening, we confirm the cabinet's back is tight to the layout line, the front is plumb, and the tops and sides are coplanar.

Make each box true. Before attaching any of the lower cabinets to the wall, we secure them to each other, then shim behind and under them as necessary to make the fronts plumb.

String ensures straight. A stringline along the top front edge of the cabinet run allows us to double-check for straightness before final fastening. Here, the string revealed a slightly bowed wall, which we easily compensated for by readjusting some of the shims.

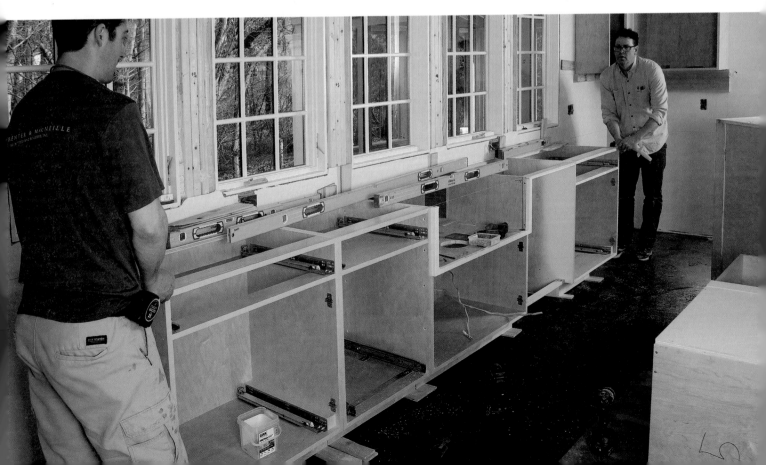

Spacers keep square. These cabinets came with finished spacers for the fronts of corners; we install a second spacer, cut from framing stock, at the back to help ensure the corners are square.

Adjust for out-of-square. When dealing with out-of-square corners, the corner cabinets must be ordered a bit undersize, leaving room to bring the box into square in spite of the wall conditions.

'Round the bend. As long as the last cabinet box in the previous run was installed plumb, level, and square, the adjacent cabinet has a good starting point. The key is to keep the show side of the corner square, and let the out-of-square conditions remain hidden behind, at the wall.

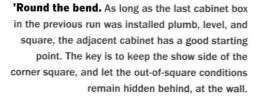

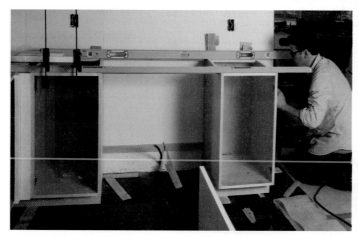

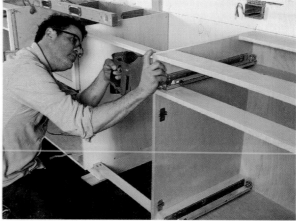

Make room for appliances. Leaving gaps for appliances is more than just measuring the width and creating a void. It's crucial that the cabinets on both sides of the gap are aligned at the top—not just at the front edge, but all the way back to the wall—and coplanar in the front. If we get this part wrong, we'll regret it when it comes time to install the countertops and appliances. We use clamps and multiple levels, and pocket-screw temporary spacers to keep things consistent.

Building islands

The locations of kitchen islands are determined during the design phase and shown on the plans. They are usually positioned parallel to a bank of cabinets and are typically the same height as the base cabinets. Islands are often centered on some feature—in this case on the sink, but it could be a window, light fixture, or appliance that provides the reference point. Once we've located and marked the center and one side of the island's location on the floor, we measure from those spots to establish its whole footprint, which we mark with yellow tape. Using the plans as a guide, we write individual cabinet and appliance locations on the tape.

Find your island. We measure from the parallel bank of cabinets in two spots to mark one side of the island, and extend the center reference point with long levels and a square.

Laser check. We set up a laser level and measure up to it in multiple places on the island's perimeter to determine if there are high spots that require trimming the cabinet bottoms to keep them in plane with the lower cabinets.

Mark for blocking. With the island cabinets screwed together and on their backs, we mark the locations of the cabinet sides for floor-mounted blocking.

Lower the island. We drill holes for any cables and pipes and pull them through while lowering the island into place as a unit.

Check the height. A laser shows the island height in relation to the other base cabinets, so the island can be shimmed to match.

Securely fasten. After shimming the island for height and level, we fasten through the cabinet bottoms into the blocking with 2-in. flathead construction screws.

Lock down the shims. Angled screws hold the shims in position permanently, so the load of the island and its top is transferred to the floor.

Put on the panels. Large panels that hide cabinet backs and sides are held with screws driven from the inside. We miter their corners on-site with a track saw before assembling them with wood glue and a line of miter clamps.

Cap the ends

Runs of frameless cabinets almost always have some way to finish off exposed cabinet ends. This kitchen's large panels are more like wall sections, but smaller end panels are handled similarly. The first thing we do is shim the panels plumb and to the correct height so any elements—rails, base trim, and panels—align with the same elements in the rest of the kitchen. Then we scribe and cut the panels to the contour of the wall.

Trim to fit. The refrigerator cabinet was too tall to stand up in the kitchen space, so we had to trim the back corners.

Individual treatment. Oversize cabinets are made plumb and level individually because their fronts don't line up with surrounding cabinets.

Match the height. The end panels, like the cabinets, get a crown molding. The amount of exposed rail below the crown must match the same detail found on the cabinets. A level laser line shows if the panels need to be raised or lowered before scribing.

Scribe to fit. Once the end panel is shimmed to the right elevation and plumbed, we use a site-made scribing block to help achieve a tight fit against the wall. We tape a flat marking knife to the block and run the block the length of the scribe. Separating the two pieces of tape reveals a perfect scribe line.

Attach from the back.
We attach end panels with screws driven from inside the cabinet so they're not seen. Screwing through spacers ensures the cabinet box won't get distorted when the screws are tightened.

Finishing touches

After we vacuum the cabinet interiors and reinstall all of the doors and drawers, we tackle any remaining decorative elements. This kitchen has crown molding with a fascia behind it that matches the plane of the door fronts. There's also a light rail under the uppers to conceal undercabinet lighting. Once the countertops are in place, we install the appliances and the toe kick to hide the joints between cabinets in the toe space.

Fascia first. A 5/4-in.-thick fascia fills the space above the cabinet doors. The parts are cut, glued, and fastened with 18-ga. brads before they're fastened to the uppers.

Crown comes next. Crown-molding corner joints can be finicky to cut and fit in place. Instead, we cut, glue, and pin these parts on a flat surface, then install them in sections.

Light rail last. Joints are coated with wood glue and a squirt of CA glue for a quick bond. Once the light rail is assembled, we attach it to the cabinet with trim screws.

Contemporary Wall Cabinet

PHILIP MORLEY

A few years ago, I built a long cabinet with tapered sides that curved outward at the top. I made extra parts, planning to build a second identical cabinet. But when I happened to see the extra sides flipped around on my bench, I envisioned instead a smaller wall cabinet with sides that curved inward at the top. I did a rough sketch, working out the asymmetrical arrangement with one section left open, and went right to building it. Since then I've returned to build it a number of times, altering the design slightly with each version.

I usually design things and then figure out how to build them. That's what happened with the curved tapered sides. Kerf-bending them came right to mind because as an apprentice I had built stairs with curved risers, and we kerf-bent those. Then I remembered an article by David Haig ("Curved Panels for Furniture," *Fine Woodworking* #231) that discussed the technique. I followed his method closely and found it very effective; the main change I made was in blocking up the tapered core to make kerfing simpler.

I think of this cabinet as having a slightly Japanese teahouse feeling: as something to make you feel good when you walk into the room. It's a place you might want to display or store favorite pieces of craft or other keepsakes. With that in mind, I leave the drawers without stays, so you can pull them right out of the case to examine what's inside (and perhaps even get a closer look at their dovetails).

Kerfing the cores

The heart of this cabinet's design is its curved and tapered sides. I make them by kerf-bending a core of solid poplar and then veneering over it with shopsawn ash. Because I use some of the same veneer for edging, the finished sides really have the look of solid ash. And because the core is solid wood, I can make the other case parts from solid wood and they'll all move together.

Before I begin kerfing, I make an over-wide poplar blank and taper it on a jig in the planer. Then I rip two strips off the blank, turn them end for end, and adhere them to

First taper the core. Morley runs his poplar core stock through the planer on a ramped jig. The blank is oversize both in length and width.

Curve-Sided Cabinet

All parts are ash, except where noted.

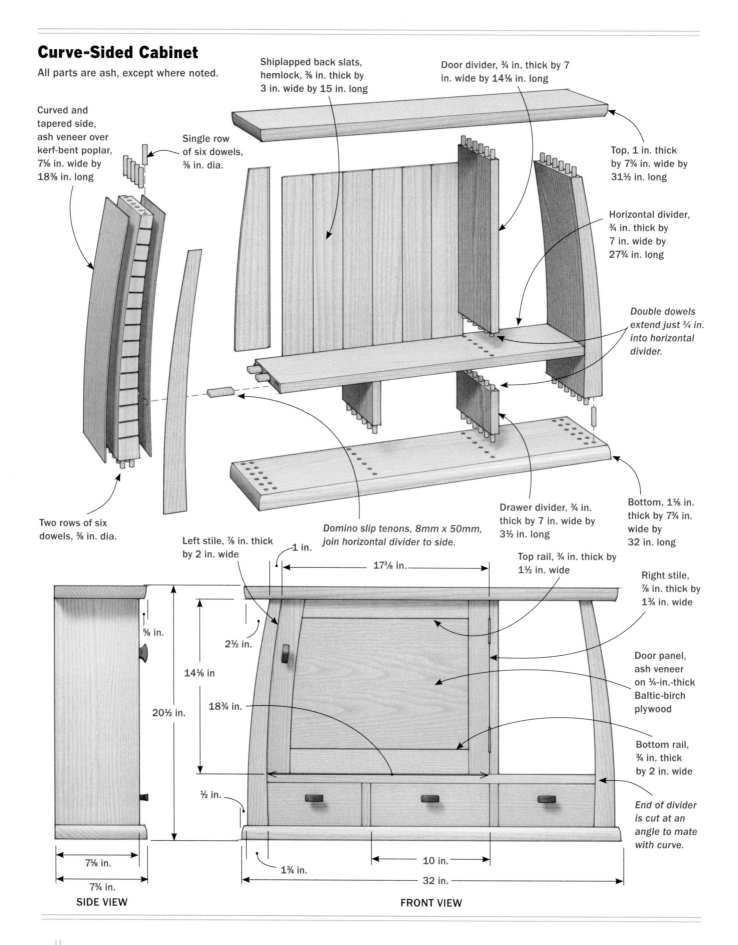

Curved and tapered side, ash veneer over kerf-bent poplar, 7⅛ in. wide by 18⅜ in. long

Single row of six dowels, ⅜ in. dia.

Shiplapped back slats, hemlock, ⅜ in. thick by 3 in. wide by 15 in. long

Door divider, ¾ in. thick by 7 in. wide by 14⅛ in. long

Top, 1 in. thick by 7¾ in. wide by 31½ in. long

Horizontal divider, ¾ in. thick by 7 in. wide by 27¾ in. long

Double dowels extend just ¼ in. into horizontal divider.

Two rows of six dowels, ⅜ in. dia.

Domino slip tenons, 8mm x 50mm, join horizontal divider to side.

Drawer divider, ¾ in. thick by 7 in. wide by 3½ in. long

Bottom, 1⅛ in. thick by 7¾ in. wide by 32 in. long

Left stile, ⅞ in. thick by 2 in. wide

Top rail, ¾ in. thick by 1½ in. wide

Right stile, ⅞ in. thick by 1¾ in. wide

Door panel, ash veneer on ¼-in.-thick Baltic-birch plywood

Bottom rail, ¾ in. thick by 2 in. wide

End of divider is cut at an angle to mate with curve.

1 in.

17⅜ in.

2½ in.

⅝ in.

14⅛ in

20½ in.

18¾ in.

½ in.

7⅛ in.

7¾ in.

1¾ in.

10 in.

32 in.

SIDE VIEW

FRONT VIEW

Rip a pair of wedges. To simplify the kerfing process, make your core blank overwide and, after tapering it, rip a wedge-shaped strip off each edge.

Reverse the wedges and tape them to the blank. Using double-sided tape, attach the tapered strips to the tapered core with their thick end at the core's thin end. Apply clamp pressure briefly along the strip to be sure the tape's grip is firm.

Cut kerfs in the core. With the inside face of the core facedown and the blade raised to within ⅛ in. of the outside face, Morley uses a dedicated sled to cut the slots that will allow the core to bend (above). After cutting all the kerfs, remove what remains of the wedges (right) and scrape off any residue from the tape.

the blank. Doing this takes a lot of fussiness out of the kerfing process. Typically, when kerf-bending a tapered part, you need to readjust the blade height after every kerf you cut. But with the two tapered strips beneath the workpiece, I can cut all the kerfs with the blade at the same height, then just remove the strips.

Bend and veneer the sides

Once the core is kerfed, it's super flexible, so bending is a breeze. I made the bending form from ¾-in. plywood. It has six ribs that are curved along one edge; I used small plywood blocks at each end to space the ribs apart. To make the ribs identical I first made a master rib by sawing and sanding to a line, then used that to template-rout the other ribs. After gluing and stapling the ribs and spacer blocks

Veneering the core. Morley glues shopsawn ash veneer to both the inside and outside faces of the poplar core. He sliced the veneers from a riftsawn ash board and milled them to ³⁄₃₂ in. To get the full width of the side, he edge-glued two veneers.

together, I covered the curved face of the form with a piece of ¼-in. Masonite.

When I was ready to do the bend, I used stretch wrap to clamp my front and back veneers to the core and then used more of it to clamp that sandwich to the bending form. Then I put the whole package into the vacuum bag.

Once it was cured, I cut the core to width and glued on the edge veneers. Crosscutting the completed sides to length was a little tricky, since there were no flat reference surfaces to work from. I laid out the cuts in pencil and used support blocks to elevate and stabilize the workpiece at just the right position for the cut.

Clear clamps. Bind the veneer tightly to the core with stretch wrap, and then wrap the whole thing to the bending form.

Gaining an atmospheric advantage. Morley puts the wrapped package—core and bending form—into his vacuum bag to apply final, even clamping pressure.

Clean the curved edges. Once the kerfed bend is cured, joint one edge (left). With the convex side down and the jointed edge against the tablesaw fence, rip the side to width (above).

Size up the edging. With the pencil's tip spaced away slightly, Morley traces the curves of the side onto a sheet of veneer. Before gluing on the edging, he cuts to the lines at the bandsaw.

Trim the perimeter. After gluing, Morley cuts off the excess edging at the router table with a flush-trimming bit. He'll tune up that trimming later with a handplane or scraper.

Custom crosscuts. With scrap blocks tucked underneath to support the side, Morley adjusts the blocks and the workpiece until his layout line is parallel to the square and aligned with the path of the blade, then makes the cut.

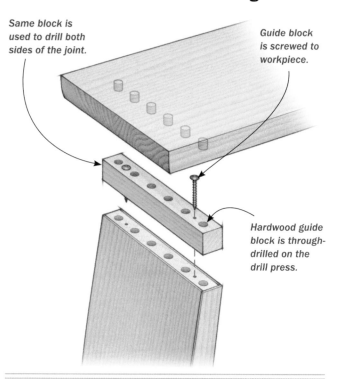

Dowel Blocks Guide the Drilling

Same block is used to drill both sides of the joint.

Guide block is screwed to workpiece.

Hardwood guide block is through-drilled on the drill press.

Drilling for dowels. After screwing the guide block in place on the bottom end of the side, Morley drills two lines of six holes with a ⅜-in. titanium twist bit. Afterward he removes the jig and uses a chamfer bit to break the edge of each hole. To drill for the dowels in the top of the side, he uses a different guide block, with just one row of holes (see drawing at right).

Spacer aligns the jig. To cut mating holes in the cabinet bottom, Morley uses the block with two rows of holes, aligning it with a long spacer (which is centered on the bottom) and an additional small spacer (right). To cut holes for the dowels that will link the side with the cabinet top (far right), Morley uses the narrower guide block. He uses the same long spacer but does not need the small spacer.

The case comes together

I used dowels for nearly all the case joints, making three different doweling blocks to guide the drilling. Where the horizontal divider meets the case sides, however, registering doweling blocks would have been complicated because of the curve, so I chose to cut Domino joints there. For the cuts into the side I built a quick L-shaped riser to hold the Domino level and at the right height. I also taped a straight scrap to the Domino's fence so that it would seat squarely against the cabinet side.

Dominos, not dowels. Where the horizontal divider meets the curved sides, Morley uses Domino joints instead of dowels. For mortising into the side, he builds a right-angle platform to support the machine (left). And since the curved top of the Domino's fence won't seat squarely against the curving cabinet side, he attaches a straight scrap to the fence with double-sided tape. For mortising into the ends of the horizontal divider (right), a long piece of stock beneath the workpiece provides easy registration.

Suss out the assembly sequence. Using just a few dowels in each joint, Morley does a dry assembly, first connecting the drawer dividers to the horizontal divider, then adding the sides, and then the bottom.

Bringing it all together. After the dry-fit, Morley disassembles the case, masks off the joinery with tape, sprays finish on the parts, and advances to the glue-up.

Rout a rabbet for the back.
To simplify rabbeting for the back, Morley waits until after final assembly and does the job with the whole cabinet riding on the router table. Before routing, he flushes up all the joints on the back of the case.

Curved door and drawer match the side

Getting the frame-and-panel door, with its curved left stile, to fit snugly to the curve of the cabinet side takes a little doing. I use a pair of nesting Masonite templates to guide the process.

First I make a template to the shape the left stile will be. I cut a piece of Masonite to the full height of the door opening and set it in place. Then I use a compass, opened a couple of inches, to follow the curve of the cabinet side while tracing onto the template. After sawing and sanding to the line, I cut a parallel curve 2 in. away on the right edge of the template. Then I make the second tem-

plate, with a convex curve that is a perfect mate for the concave curve of the first template. These two templates guide the layout and trim routing for the left stile, the two rails, and the door panel. It's important to note that the mortises for the slip tenons that join the door frame are cut while the rails and stiles are still square.

Making the left and right drawers match the curve of the sides is far simpler. I make the drawer boxes with one side extra thick and then shape that side to the curve at a stationary belt sander, or else with a handplane.

Marking the rails. Using the narrow template, Morley lays out the curved crosscuts on the left end of the rails.

Templates Shape the Door Parts

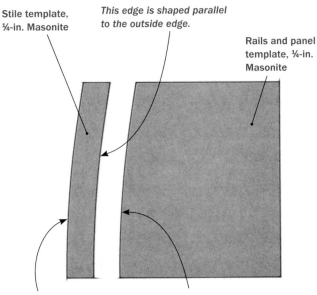

Stile template, ¼-in. Masonite

This edge is shaped parallel to the outside edge.

Rails and panel template, ¼-in. Masonite

This edge is shaped to fit the curve of the case.

This edge is shaped to match the inside edge of the stile template.

Template-rout the stile. After routing mortises for slip tenons and then bandsawing the door stile's curved inner edge, Morley template-routs the curve to finished shape.

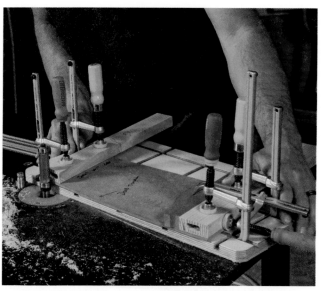

Rails get a trim, too. After cutting the mortises in the rails, Morley routs the ends to a curve, following the wide template. The rails are attached to the template with double-sided tape and firmly clamped to the sled.

Curve the panel. The door panel, a ¼-in. Baltic-birch plywood substrate veneered with ash on both faces, gets trimmed to final shape with the large template. The template is adhered to the panel with double-sided tape.

The door's last curve. Having parallel edges is a clamping advantage, so Morley waits until after the door is glued up to bandsaw out the door stile's outer curve. He'll dial in its fit to the cabinet side with a stationary belt sander and hand tools.

Intentional asymmetry. Morley builds the cabinet's left drawer with its left side overthick. Having shaped a piece of ¼-in. MDF to the curve of the drawer pocket, he transfers the curve onto the drawer. He does the same with the right drawer.

Shape to the line. Rocking the drawer side against a belt sander does a smooth job of creating a curved side to match the cabinet.

Half-blind dovetails, after the fact. Once the drawer side is fitted to the curved drawer pocket, Morley glues a piece of ash veneer to the front, converting through-dovetails into half-blinds. He builds the other two drawers the same way.

Final trim. Once the glue has cured, the front veneer can be flush-trimmed to the drawer box.

Wall Cabinet
with Curves

CLARK KELLOGG

This cabinet was my first big project as a student in the *Fine Woodworking* program at the College of the Redwoods. My inspiration was a cabinet-on-stand made by James Krenov, which I was fortunate to see in person. Although the cabinet is modest in size, I was struck by its subtle details, flawless proportions, and balanced exploration of form: a restrained exterior matched with a playfully arranged interior. So, when I was told to build something "small, simple, solid, and sweet," I built this little wall-hung cabinet, which I hope captures what I admired in Krenov's cabinet but expresses it in a slightly different manner.

Wall Cabinet in Beech

Refined details and an asymmetric curve combine to give this cabinet a rich, contemporary beauty.

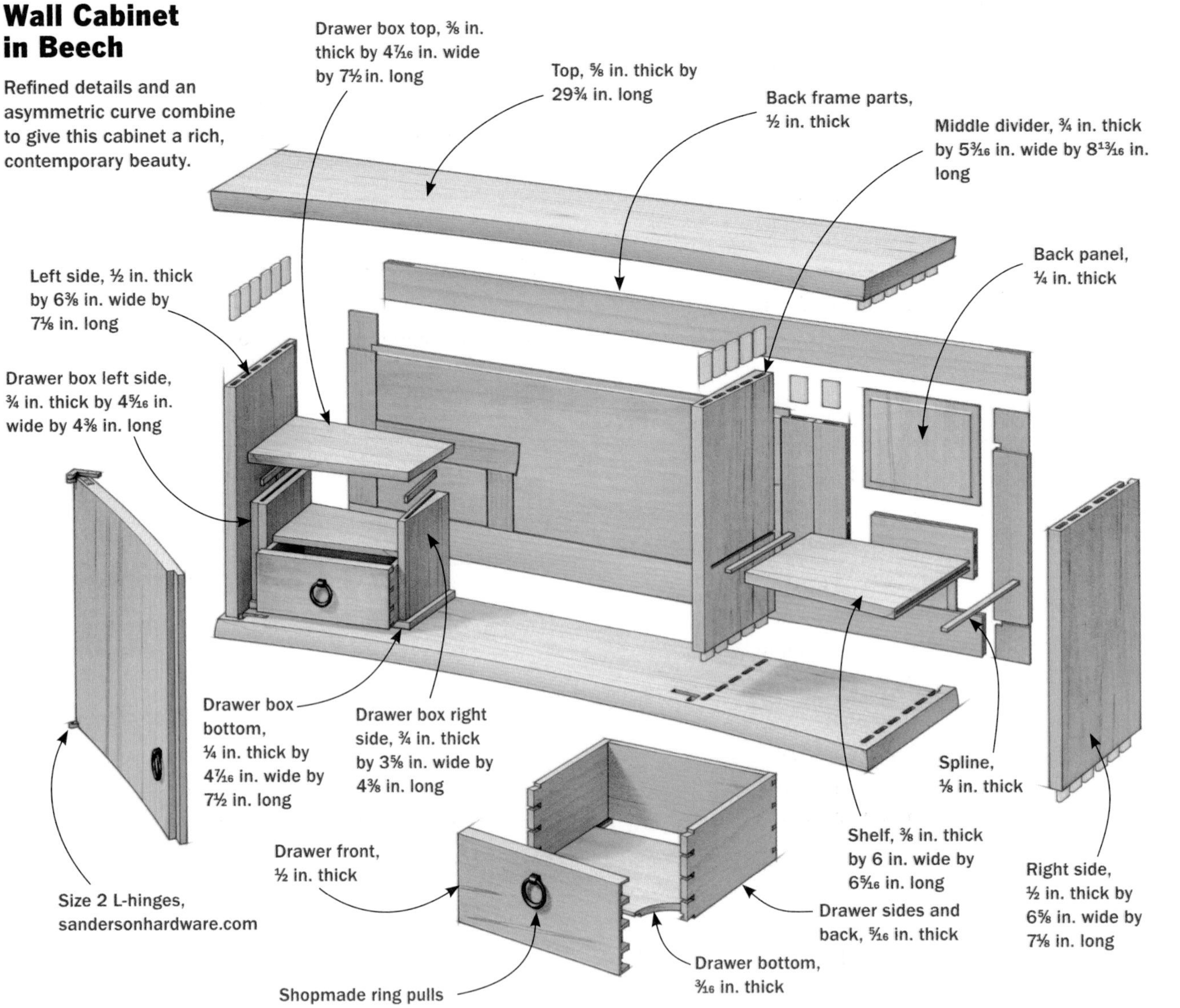

Drawer box top, 3/8 in. thick by 4 7/16 in. wide by 7 1/2 in. long
Top, 5/8 in. thick by 29 3/4 in. long
Back frame parts, 1/2 in. thick
Middle divider, 3/4 in. thick by 5 3/16 in. wide by 8 13/16 in. long
Back panel, 1/4 in. thick
Left side, 1/2 in. thick by 6 3/8 in. wide by 7 7/8 in. long
Drawer box left side, 3/4 in. thick by 4 5/16 in. wide by 4 3/8 in. long
Drawer box bottom, 1/4 in. thick by 4 7/16 in. wide by 7 1/2 in. long
Drawer box right side, 3/4 in. thick by 3 5/8 in. wide by 4 3/8 in. long
Spline, 1/8 in. thick
Shelf, 3/8 in. thick by 6 in. wide by 6 5/16 in. long
Right side, 1/2 in. thick by 6 5/8 in. wide by 7 7/8 in. long
Drawer front, 1/2 in. thick
Drawer sides and back, 5/16 in. thick
Size 2 L-hinges, sandersonhardware.com
Drawer bottom, 3/16 in. thick
Shopmade ring pulls

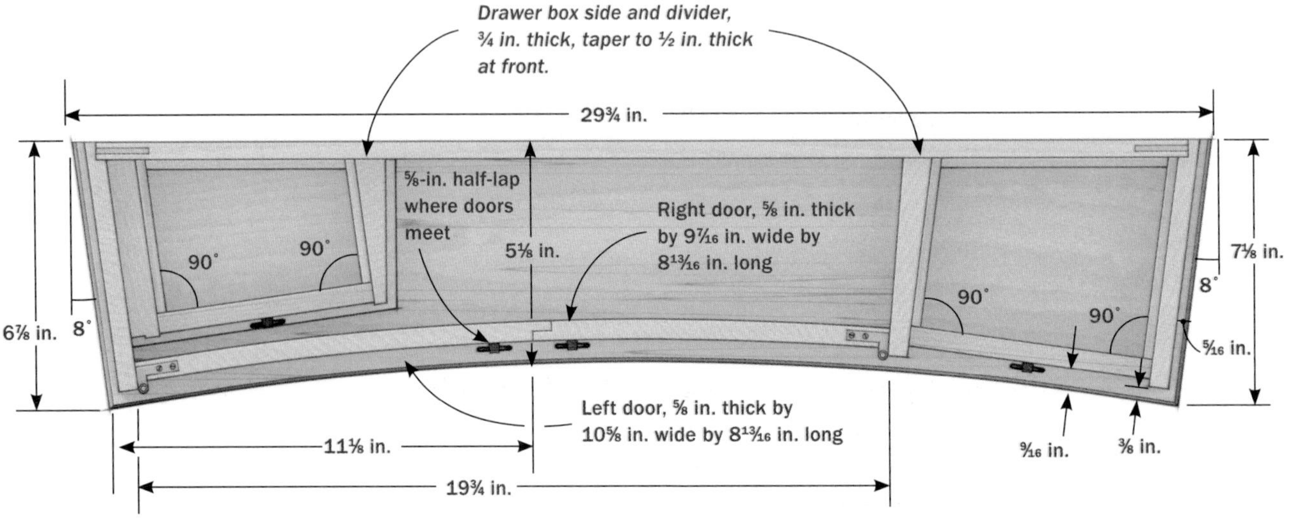

Drawer box side and divider, 3/4 in. thick, taper to 1/2 in. thick at front.
29 3/4 in.
5/8-in. half-lap where doors meet
5 1/8 in.
Right door, 5/8 in. thick by 9 7/16 in. wide by 8 13/16 in. long
90°
90°
90°
90°
6 7/8 in.
8°
8°
7 7/8 in.
5/16 in.
Left door, 5/8 in. thick by 10 5/8 in. wide by 8 13/16 in. long
11 1/8 in.
19 3/4 in.
9/16 in.
3/8 in.

There are a few elements of this cabinet that seem tricky—curved doors, tapered dividers, and an intricate frame-and-panel back—but building it is fairly straightforward. The carcase is joined with slip tenons, and the back is made with bridle joints and slip tenons. The doors, which are made from slabs of solid wood, have a subtle curve created with handplanes. A matching curve is cut into the cabinet's top and bottom.

Use planes to curve the doors

I began with the doors rather than the cabinet, and there's a good reason for it. It's much easier to adjust the curve on the front edge of the cabinet's top and bottom to match the doors than it would be to adjust the doors to match the cabinet.

The doors are made from solid wood, and because they are wider than they are tall, you might think that they could warp into pretzels or expand to the point of locking themselves shut. But don't worry. They're made from quartersawn boards (riftsawn works, too), so there's very little seasonal movement. Also, the doors are fully inset into the cabinet, which means that they don't need to lie flat against a frame. And the little warping that will occur won't be noticeable because both the front and back faces of the doors are curved.

To begin making the doors, create a full-size pattern. Next, mill two door blanks, leaving them about ¼ in. longer than their final dimension, and a bit wider, too.

Plane the front of the first door to create its concave curve. I use a shopmade coopering plane for this. Work your way across the door's face, checking your progress against the curve drawn on the end grain. Keep an eye on the door's thickness at the top and bottom to keep it consistent. When you plane the second door, check it against the

first door to ensure that the transition from one to the other is smooth. Don't worry too much if the curve is not perfect. As long as it's a gentle, fair curve, they'll look great.

After the fronts of the doors are complete, flip them over and shape the backs. Because the curve is convex, the shaping can be done with any normal bench plane. As the blanks start to get thinner, you may need to make some curved supports to keep the doors from flexing as you plane them.

Next, cut the rabbets on the doors. You will need to prop up the doors as you run them across the router table to accommodate their respective curves. Sneak up on the fit, sliding the doors together after each pass. The rabbets should overlap so that there is no break in the curve as it travels from one door to the other.

Build the cabinet around the doors

The cabinet's top and bottom are curved along their front edges. The drawer box side and middle divider are tapered in thickness, being thicker at the back of the cabinet than at the front. This allows them to be

Make the doors first. It's far less work to adjust the curve on the cabinet's top and bottom to match the doors than it would be to adjust the doors to match the cabinet. Use a template to create the curve and trace it onto both ends of the door blank. Because it changes radius over its length, Kellogg uses a complete template of the curve. The other half is for the second door.

Hollow the front. With the help of a coopering plane, dish out the door's outside face, working with the grain.

Curve the back. Working with a coopering plane, cut across the grain first to remove material quickly (shown), then use a flat-sole plane along the grain to refine the door's shape.

Doors meet with a rabbet. One door gets a rabbet on its front, the other on its back. Use a block to raise the door so that the rabbet is square to the door's edge.

parallel to the ends of the top and bottom on the outside face, but square to the back on the inside face. The joinery that holds the case and drawer box together is cut before these parts are shaped, which makes the construction far simpler than if the joints were cut afterward.

Mill the parts to their final dimension, leaving the top and bottom long and the sides about ⅛ in. wider than their final width. Next, lay out the mortise locations on the sides and divider. Because I used a Domino joiner to cut the mortises for this project, I marked only the centerline for each mortise. I marked the centerlines on the end grain and then transferred them to the panel's face. After cutting the mortises, assemble the case dry, using a few slip tenons per joint.

Fit the doors

The doors swing on offset knife hinges (L-hinges, size 2, sandersonhardware. com), and the space between the hinges and the cabinet sides is extremely narrow, the thickness of a piece of blue tape. So, put a piece of tape on the cabinet side (top left

Slip tenons join the case. Plenty strong enough for this wall cabinet, slip tenons also make it easy to join sides to an overhanging top and bottom. To mortise the sides Kellogg uses a Festool Domino joiner, which speeds up and simplifies the joinery. A doweling jig and dowels can be used instead of Dominoes.

Use the side as a guide. Place the side down parallel, but inset from, its location in the assembled cabinet (above). After clamping it down, use it as a fence for the Domino joiner, aligning the tool with the layout lines on the cabinet side to create mating mortises (right).

photo, p. 146). The center of the hinge pin should line up with the front edge of the cabinet side.

When you have the hinge leaf in place, scribe around it with a knife. Repeat for the other three hinges. Disassemble the cabinet and rout away the waste freehand, using a trim router and ⅛-in. straight bit. Set the depth of cut so the hinges sit about ¹⁄₃₂ in. below the surface to allow for planing or sanding the surface. Carefully pare to the scribe lines with a sharp chisel.

Next, reassemble the case (still without glue). Plane the doors to fit. Remove material from the top, bottom, and outside edges, but not from the inside edge. Across their width, they should just fit inside the case. Mortise the hinges into the top and bottom of each door. After transferring the mortise location from the cabinet to the door, rout and pare the mortises in the same manner as before.

After the doors are swinging and the rabbets are overlapping correctly, clamp a pair of sticks inside the cabinet to act as stops. Then, with the doors closed, trace a line ½ in. offset and parallel to the doors' curve onto the carcase top and bottom. Because the curve of the two doors may differ from your original drawing, it is better to adapt the shape of the cabinet to the doors you have made, rather than trying to go back and re-shape the doors. Bandsaw and

The doors swing on knife hinges. Barely visible when installed, knife hinges are perfect for a cabinet with modern lines. Use offset, or L-shape, hinges so that the inset door swings open as far as possible. Start by locating the hinge. Blue tape on the cabinet creates a perfect gap, while a combination square ensures that all the hinges are in the same plane.

Knife the layout. Holding the leaf in place with a finger, cut around the perimeter to define the mortise.

Pare to fit. After routing out the waste, use a chisel to clean up to the layout lines.

Mortise the door. Locate the door in the cabinet. Clamp scraps in the cabinet to keep it in place (left). Slide the door over and transfer the mortise (above left). Hold the hinge in place and cut around it (above right).

spokeshave the case pieces to shape (see photos on the facing page. I use a spokeshave to give the edges a slightly elliptical profile.

Now it's time to taper the right-hand face of the middle divider. I scribe a line on the front edge of the divider marking its final thickness, and then use a handplane to remove the waste. Work back and forth across the grain, taking more shavings where it's thinner, until the divider is tapered to its final dimensions.

Make a drawer pocket, then assemble the case

The shelf that serves as the top of the right-hand drawer pocket is held in place with splines, which means that the middle divider, the case side, and the shelf need dadoes. I start with the stopped dadoes in the case parts, using a straightedge clamped to the workpiece to guide a small router that's spinning a ⅛-in.-dia. spiral bit.

Next up are the grooves in the shelf. It's important that the shelf fits without gaps between the case side and middle divider, so cut it a bit long and then sneak up on the fit, using a shooting board and block plane to carefully trim the length until it just slides into place. After the shelf has been fitted, rout grooves in the ends using the same ⅛-in.-dia. bit used to rout the dadoes. I do this at the router table, standing the shelf on end and pressed against the fence.

Next, mill up some ⅛-in.-thick spline stock using the same material you used for the cabinet. Note that the grain of the splines runs parallel to the grain of the shelf. This may seem counterintuitive, as you will end up with splines that are ¼ in. long by 6 in. wide; however, if you were to run the grain lengthwise you would run into serious wood movement issues.

Now cut the rabbets that will accept the back panel. I use a rabbeting bit in the router table, then cut the top and bottom to length, and do any shaping and smoothing necessary. I also prefinish all the parts—once the case goes together, getting a nice finish in the corners is tricky.

When gluing up the cabinet, use clamping cauls to distribute pressure evenly across its depth. After the glue is dry, use a chisel to square up the stopped ends of the rabbets in the cabinet.

Elegant back encloses the cabinet

The frame-and-panel back has an outer frame held together with bridle joints and inner frame members joined to it with slip tenons. I cut the bridle joints on the bandsaw and with a crosscut sled on the tablesaw. Make the frame about ¹⁄₁₆ in. oversize in total height and width. The internal frame members are joined with Dominoes.

Next, shape the end of the short horizontal frame piece to match the profile on the

Complete the case. The curve along the front edge of the cabinet should match the arc of the doors, so take care when cleaning up after cutting the curve at the bandsaw. Do the curve along the front edge first, staying close to the layout line (left), then cut both ends (below). There is no need to do this at the tablesaw because the cut will be cleaned up in the next step.

Take a spokeshave to the edge. It's a quick way to remove the machine marks, refine the curve, and create the edge profile. Do the same for the end grain.

Glue up the case. Glue the sides and middle divider into the bottom, then add the top. After gluing the splines into the shelf, spread glue in the dadoes and push in the shelf from behind.

Spline joins the shelf and cabinet. The side needs a dado. Cut it with a router guided by a straightedge (top). Use the same bit at the router table to rout a groove in the shelf's end grain (center). The grain of the spline should run in the same direction as the grain of the shelf to prevent problems from wood movement (bottom).

outside of the cabinet. I used a block plane, but a disk sander would also work. Disassemble the frame and cut the grooves for the panels into the frame pieces with a ⅛-in. three-wing slot-cutter (Whiteside Machine Co., No. 1906) on the router table.

Reassemble the frame and trace the inside of each section (there should be four) on a

Framed with a Flourish

Sure, you could use a simple frame-and-panel back, but making one that follows the cabinet's lines, including the interior drawers, is far more attractive and interesting.

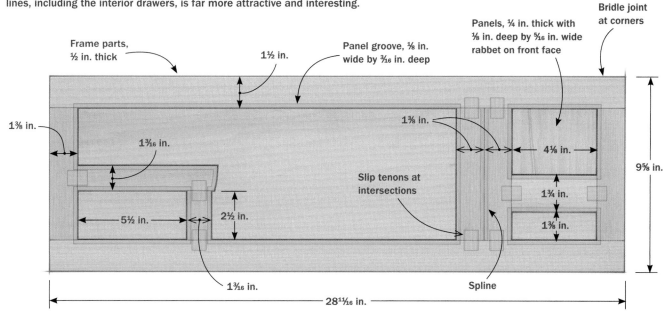

Frame parts, ½ in. thick

1½ in.

Panel groove, ⅛ in. wide by ⅜₁₆ in. deep

Panels, ¼ in. thick with ⅛ in. deep by ⁵⁄₁₆ in. wide rabbet on front face

Bridle joint at corners

1⅜ in.

1¾₁₆ in.

1⅜ in.

4⅛ in.

9⅝ in.

Slip tenons at intersections

5½ in.

2½ in.

1¾ in.

1⅜ in.

1¾₁₆ in.

Spline

28¹¹⁄₁₆ in.

piece of ¼-in.-thick solid stock (top photos, p. 150). Remove the frame and draw a new set of lines outside the traced lines, offset exactly ³⁄₁₆ in. Cut out the panels. Next, use a straight bit to rabbet the panels. Again, sneak up on the fit—you don't want the panel to crack the frame, but you don't want it to rattle around, either.

Cutting the rabbet on the notched section of the larger panel can get a little tricky, because you need to replace your normal fence with one that comes to a point so that you can get into the tight corners. However, because the bit won't get all the way into the corner, you will need to use chisels to square up the round left by the router bit. Do your best to maintain the rabbet's radiused corner. Reassemble the frame and install the panels to check how everything fits, then smooth and prefinish the panels before gluing up the assembly.

Once the glue has dried, plane or sand the joints of the frame flush and use a

block plane to begin fitting the frame to the back rabbet.

If the cabinet or frame is out of square, plane the frame to fit by starting in one corner of the frame, then working out along the two adjacent edges until the corner of the back panel fits into its respective corner of the rabbet. Next, plane the remaining two edges to fit. The fit of the back panel should be snug, but not overly tight. You really don't want to break your cabinet apart at this point (or at any other point, for that matter.)

Next, sand and finish the frame, then glue the back panel assembly into the case. You don't need much glue, or much pressure on the panel, and you don't want to damage the profiled front edges of the cabinet. Wooden cam clamps, with their moderate grip and forgiving jaws, work great for this job.

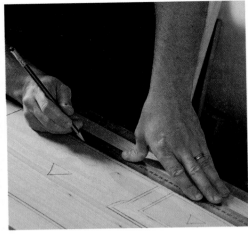

Trace the frame. Assemble the frame dry and lay it down (front face up) on an oversize blank. Transfer all of the inside edges to the blank. Then lay out offset lines to account for the tongues that fit into the frame groove.

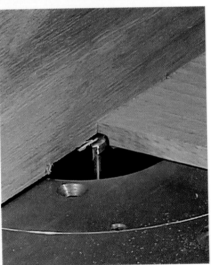

Cut out the panels and rabbet the edges. Cut out the individual panels at the bandsaw. Kellogg uses a straight bit to create a rabbet with a soft corner. A pointy fence gets into the tight corner. The fence's point is offset from the bit's outside edge.

Three parts at once. Join the two small frame parts, and then hold them in place beneath the panel. Slide the panel into the groove, guiding the slip tenon on the small rail into its mating mortise (top). The last panel fits in from the side (above). Finally, glue the last frame part in place (right).

Wall Cabinet with Simple Joinery

MICHAEL PEKOVICH

This quick project is a great example of how building with basic joinery doesn't mean limiting the design possibilities or the strength of the construction. Rabbets and dadoes are common to just about everything we make, but they are most often seen as a supporting cast to the more powerful mortise-and-tenons and sophisticated dovetail joinery. That said, used in combination, rabbets and dadoes are a fast and versatile way to build. They are also simple to cut, which makes them a good choice for both hand and machine work. If you told me that I could only use rabbets and dadoes in my work, I think I could build a lot of projects before running out of ideas.

On this cabinet the sides and back boards extend beyond the top and bottom shelves, allowing them to be profiled for a light, fun look. Along with a curve at the top, there's a cove at the bottom that creates a space for a narrow exposed shelf for odds and ends. This is my favorite detail of the piece.

Vertical stiles glued to the front of the case serve as a partial face frame. Visually they add mass to the piece by hiding the narrow front edge of the sides, and they conceal the through-dadoes for the shelves. They are also an important structural element, tying the sides to the shelves and adding strength to the dado joints. The door itself consists of pinned half-lap joints at the corners with applied edging to house the mirror. The back

Mirrored Wall Cabinet

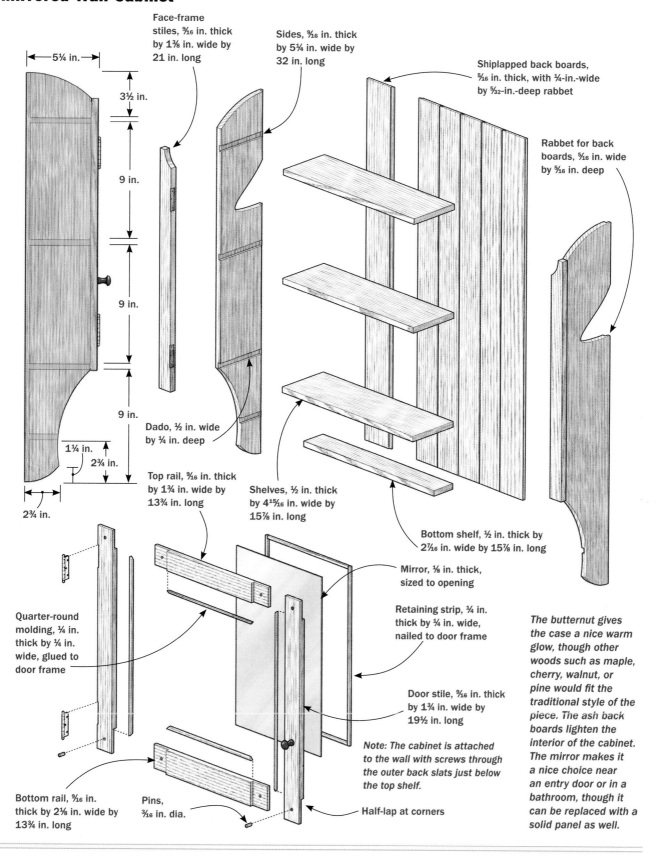

5¼ in.

3½ in.

9 in.

9 in.

9 in.

1¼ in.

2¾ in.

2¾ in.

Face-frame stiles, ⁹⁄₁₆ in. thick by 1⅜ in. wide by 21 in. long

Sides, ⁹⁄₁₆ in. thick by 5¼ in. wide by 32 in. long

Shiplapped back boards, ⁵⁄₁₆ in. thick, with ¼-in.-wide by ⁵⁄₃₂-in.-deep rabbet

Rabbet for back boards, ⁵⁄₁₆ in. wide by ⁵⁄₁₆ in. deep

Dado, ½ in. wide by ¼ in. deep

Top rail, ⁹⁄₁₆ in. thick by 1¾ in. wide by 13¾ in. long

Shelves, ½ in. thick by 4¹⁵⁄₁₆ in. wide by 15⅞ in. long

Bottom shelf, ½ in. thick by 2⁷⁄₁₆ in. wide by 15⅞ in. long

Mirror, ⅛ in. thick, sized to opening

Retaining strip, ¼ in. thick by ¼ in. wide, nailed to door frame

Quarter-round molding, ¼ in. thick by ¼ in. wide, glued to door frame

Door stile, ⁹⁄₁₆ in. thick by 1¾ in. wide by 19½ in. long

The butternut gives the case a nice warm glow, though other woods such as maple, cherry, walnut, or pine would fit the traditional style of the piece. The ash back boards lighten the interior of the cabinet. The mirror makes it a nice choice near an entry door or in a bathroom, though it can be replaced with a solid panel as well.

Note: The cabinet is attached to the wall with screws through the outer back slats just below the top shelf.

Bottom rail, ⁹⁄₁₆ in. thick by 2⅛ in. wide by 13¾ in. long

Pins, ³⁄₁₆ in. dia.

Half-lap at corners

slats also help tie the sides to the shelves at the back of the case and are rabbeted or "shiplapped" where they meet to allow for seasonal movement without creating gaps between the boards. All of these represent smart building solutions that you can put to use on any project design.

Fast case construction with rabbets and dadoes

It's important that the dadoes on the two case sides are aligned. One way to get consistent results is to use an end stop on a crosscut sled. Another solution, which works for narrower parts, is to cut both at once. That's what I did here.

Line it up. Place the parts side by side with their ends aligned and stretch tape across the joint in a few locations (left). This does a good job of keeping the sides in alignment during the cut. Using this method, all you need to do is mark the dado locations on the edge of one piece and align the pencil marks with the kerf in the crosscut sled (right).

You can't miss. Because both parts are cut at once, the dadoes will line up even if you miss your mark. This is why a pencil mark is fine, and it lets you skip the stop blocks. When dadoing two pieces at once, it's important to keep the stock flat on the sled. A push pad spanning both parts works well.

Dial in the fit. The final joinery task on the case is to rabbet the sides for the back boards (left). To dial in the thickness of the shelves, use a test piece dadoed like the sides to gauge your progress at the planer (right).

A bit snug. I aim for a fit that's a little too snug, which gives me a chance to plane the parts without creating a gap in the joint.

Add some curves. Once the joinery is cut, you can saw and smooth the profiles at the top and bottom of the case.

Get the placement right. At the back of the shelves where their edges need to be flush with the rabbet, I tape a strip of wood into the rabbet that I can use to register them against.

Avoid racking. To guarantee that the shelves align with the front of the case, I rip them slightly over width and flush them off after assembly. During glue-up, make sure the clamps are aligned over the dadoes, as it's easy to rack the case out of square if you're not paying attention.

A strategy for aligning parts during glue-up

The challenge when gluing up a through-dadoed case is to make sure the shelves are aligned front to back. I use two different methods to ensure good results.

Flush the fronts. Once the clamps come off, flush the front of the shelves with the case sides.

Glue the stiles. Finally, glue on the face-frame stiles. I cut the hinge mortises in them before assembly.

A quick lesson in making a shiplapped back

A shiplapped back consists of slats tacked or screwed to the back of the case. To allow room for seasonal movement, each board is rabbeted to overlap the adjoining one. As simple as it is, here are a couple of tips that can help you end up with a nice case back. The first challenge is calculating the width of the boards. You'll need to account for the width of the opening, the number of boards, the amount of overlap between each board, and finally the desired gap between the boards. It's a lot to keep track of, so I make a full-size drawing to ensure the numbers add up. Even then, I leave the end slats a little wide and then trim them to fit. Next, arrange the slats and mark a triangle across their backs. Now you can mark the rabbet locations on the edges of the slats.

Avoid confusion. You'll need a pair of rabbets at each joint, one on the front face of one piece and the other on the rear face of its mate. It can get a little confusing, so I mark an "O" on every edge that needs a rabbet and an "X" on those that don't. This reduces the head scratching at the tablesaw.

Keep it even. I use a pair of push pads to ensure a rabbet of even depth along the length of the slat.

Glue and nails. The end slats play an important role in strengthening the case by tying the sides to the shelves, so I glue them as well as nail them in place. The center slats are nailed at each shelf, using shims between them to maintain even spacing. For larger cases, I'd opt for screws instead of nails.

Cut the half-laps. I use a miter gauge and dado blade at the tablesaw in the same way that I would cut a tenon, but in this case there's just a single cheek to cut on each piece.

Get out the clamps. The half-lap's shortcoming as a frame joint is that it needs a lot of clamps to keep it aligned during glue-up. You'll need a pair of clamps oriented across the width of the frame and a pair along the length as well. In addition, you'll need to clamp the joint top to bottom. It's not absolutely necessary, but pinning the joint after glue-up adds mechanical strength and creates a nice visual detail.

Simple, strong door frame

A half-lap may not seem like a joint suited for a door frame. Though not commonly used, the joint can handle the job quite well. The broad glue surface of the joint makes it very strong and it's quick to make.

Make your molding. Start by routing a roundover on both edges of a wide piece of stock. Then rip a strip off of each edge to create the molding.

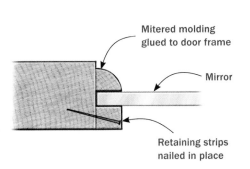

Mitered molding glued to door frame

Mirror

Retaining strips nailed in place

Mitered edging creates a seat for the mirror

Instead of rabbeting the frame for the mirror, you can create a rabbet by gluing mitered molding along the inside edge of the frame. On this piece, quarter-round molding creates a thumbnail profile when it's installed just below the frame surface.

Now add the mirror. To secure the mirror, I make square strips and nail them in place without glue. This allows the mirror to be removed later if necessary. Gluing rice paper to the back of the mirror offers a nice surprise when the door is opened.

Time to fine tune. I find the mitering and fitting of the molding is best done by hand. Saw a rough miter on each end leaving the piece overlong. Then use a handplane and shooting board to fine-tune the angle and take it to final length.

Attach the molding. Aim for a snug fit at the corners, but not so tight that the molding bows out at the center. For glue-up, I place tape-covered MDF spacers in the opening to register the molding at the right height on the frame edge. The tight miters hold the parts in place allowing you to skip the clamps.

A Better-Built Cabinet

STEVE LATTA

Rabbeted dovetails keep case square

Spacers simplify case dadoes

Clean moldings, no measuring

When selecting projects for my woodworking students, I look for pieces that will challenge them, and this wall cabinet fits the bill nicely. Many of its lessons revolve around the case joinery and molding, so I'll focus on those two aspects of this build.

My methods, using spacer blocks and setup pieces, and sizing parts to my cutters, take many of the pitfalls out of building while also streamlining the process. For example, a setup piece might take two minutes to make but save 30 minutes of fitting; or it might prevent a mistake requiring a lengthy repair. Taken together, the strategies here will have you building better, faster, and more efficiently.

Wall Cabinet

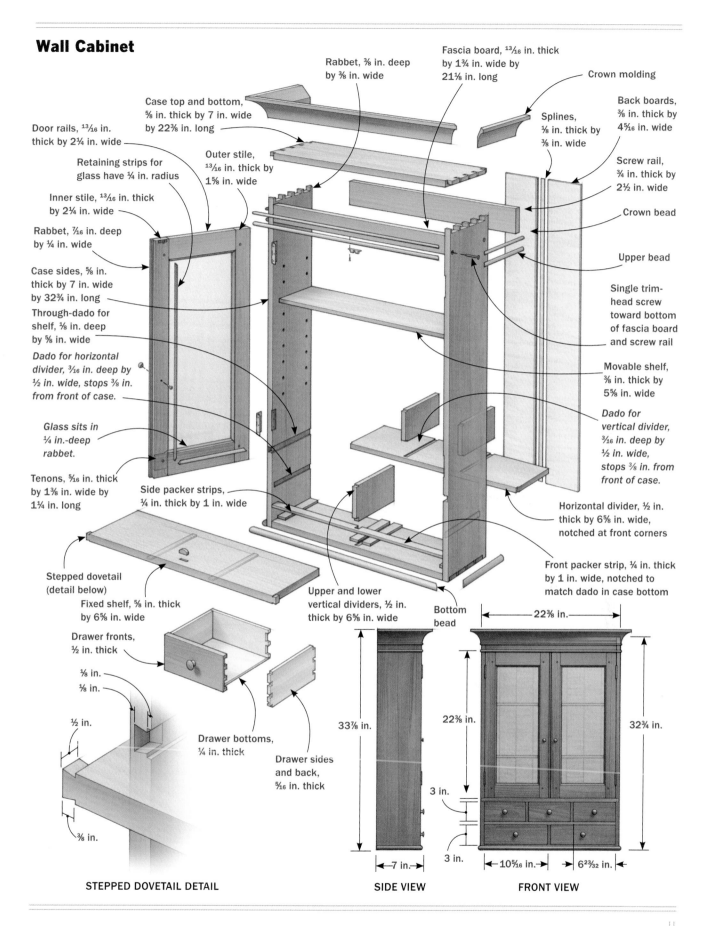

Rabbet, ⅜ in. deep by ⅜ in. wide

Fascia board, ¹³⁄₁₆ in. thick by 1¾ in. wide by 21⅛ in. long

Crown molding

Case top and bottom, ⅝ in. thick by 7 in. wide by 22⅜ in. long

Splines, ⅛ in. thick by ⅜ in. wide

Back boards, ⅜ in. thick by 4⁵⁄₁₆ in. wide

Door rails, ¹³⁄₁₆ in. thick by 2¼ in. wide

Outer stile, ¹³⁄₁₆ in. thick by 1⅝ in. wide

Screw rail, ¾ in. thick by 2½ in. wide

Retaining strips for glass have ¼ in. radius

Crown bead

Inner stile, ¹³⁄₁₆ in. thick by 2¼ in. wide

Upper bead

Rabbet, ⁷⁄₁₆ in. deep by ¼ in. wide

Single trim-head screw toward bottom of fascia board and screw rail

Case sides, ⅝ in. thick by 7 in. wide by 32¾ in. long

Through-dado for shelf, ⅛ in. deep by ⅝ in. wide

Movable shelf, ⅜ in. thick by 5⅝ in. wide

Dado for horizontal divider, ³⁄₁₆ in. deep by ½ in. wide, stops ⅜ in. from front of case.

Dado for vertical divider, ³⁄₁₆ in. deep by ½ in. wide, stops ⅜ in. from front of case.

Glass sits in ¼ in.-deep rabbet.

Horizontal divider, ½ in. thick by 6⅝ in. wide, notched at front corners

Tenons, ⁵⁄₁₆ in. thick by 1⅜ in. wide by 1¼ in. long

Side packer strips, ¼ in. thick by 1 in. wide

Front packer strip, ¼ in. thick by 1 in. wide, notched to match dado in case bottom

Stepped dovetail (detail below)

Fixed shelf, ⅝ in. thick by 6⅝ in. wide

Upper and lower vertical dividers, ½ in. thick by 6⅝ in. wide

Bottom bead

22⅜ in.

Drawer fronts, ½ in. thick

⅛ in.

⅛ in.

½ in.

Drawer bottoms, ¼ in. thick

Drawer sides and back, ⁵⁄₁₆ in. thick

22⅜ in.

32¾ in.

⅜ in.

33⅞ in.

3 in.

3 in.

7 in.

10⁵⁄₁₆ in.

6²³⁄₃₂ in.

STEPPED DOVETAIL DETAIL

SIDE VIEW

FRONT VIEW

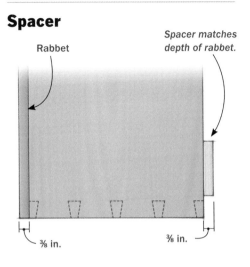

Spacer

Rabbet

Spacer matches depth of rabbet.

⅜ in.

⅜ in.

Case dovetails with rabbet. The rabbet at the back of the case calls for a spacer in the front. Cutting tablesawn dovetails is much more efficient if they're symmetrical, letting you register both edges of the board against the same stop block. To make the dovetails symmetrical on a rabbeted workpiece, Latta uses double-sided tape to attach spacer blocks to its front edge that match the depth of the rabbet.

One stop, eight cuts. With the rabbeted edge of the tail board against the stop, Latta cuts one kerf with a specialty dovetail blade, then flips the board so the spacer is against the stop and cuts again. After repeating these cuts on the other end and board, he moves the stop for a new set of cuts (right).

Strategy starts at milling

Furniture making involves a lot of test-fitting. With power tools, this often means moving a fence or blade multiple times while making test cuts as you home in on the correct setup. But doing this kind of setup on actual furniture parts is asking for trouble. I never set up machines using the actual stock. It is too easy to make a mistake, leaving me to play catchup.

Instead, I make setup pieces. I mill them at the same time and at the same settings as my workpieces. They're invaluable, saving time and leading to cleaner results. For this cabinet, make setup pieces mirroring the length and thickness of the top and bottom and the upper shelf. A 5-in. offcut from the top or bottom works great for laying out the case dovetails.

Size to your tooling as well. Don't just mill the ⅝-in.-thick main shelf to 0.625 in. on

Vertical Cut

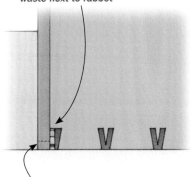

Blade at 90° to remove waste next to rabbet

Leftover tab will be trimmed to fill rabbet in pin board.

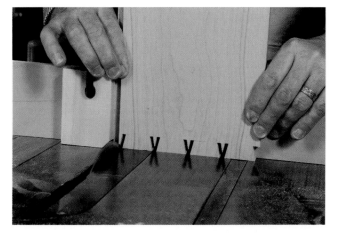

Vertical cut next to the rabbet. Latta uses a standard rip blade set to 90° to clear the waste next to the rabbet, leaving him with a thin tab to trim to length later.

Rabbet the dovetails. After cutting the shoulder, Latta installs a high fence before cutting the cheek.

Rabbet

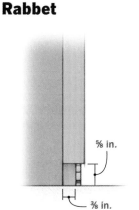

⅝ in.

⅜ in.

TIP When you rabbet the tail boards, rabbet a setup stick too. This piece is the same length as the cabinet's top and bottom. By rabbeting it with the same settings as the dovetails, you'll have a stick with an equal distance between shoulders, helping you keep the inside of the cabinet square later.

Transfer the tails.
Keeping the rabbet's shoulder tight to the pin board, Latta uses a knife to scribe the tails' shape onto the pin board.

Tab

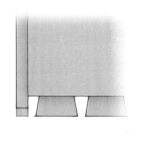

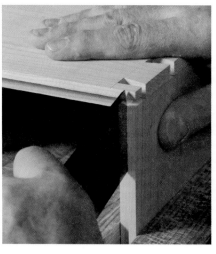

Plane blade rides rabbet to mark length of tab. This tab needs to fill the rabbet. To scribe it accurately, Latta scores it by registering a plane blade off the bottom of the rabbet (above). After that, he saws it to length (above right).

your dial indicator. Rather, because it fits in a dado that I rout, I thickness it to a sample groove cut with the actual ⅝-in. router bit. Do the same for the ½-in.-thick components.

Finally, build from the outside in using your actual case. Don't get caught up in some measured drawing. In the trade, we call this "verify in field," or VIF. It is a matter of accepting reality, not making excuses for sloppy work. For example, if you have to plane your sides slightly under ⅝ in. to get rid of roughness, do it. Later, pull dimensions, like shoulder-to-shoulder lengths, from the case itself, not a drawing, to maintain accuracy. In other words, verify in the field.

Smarter dovetails on the tablesaw

Hand-cut dovetails are an essential skill, but for cutting them on the tablesaw, I use two miter gauges with an auxiliary fence combined with a specialty dovetail blade ground to 10° (photos p. 162). When setting the height of the blade, I use an offcut with the dovetail baseline scribed onto it.

The most efficient option when cutting these tails is to lay them out symmetrically. This lets you lay out the tails on one end, set a

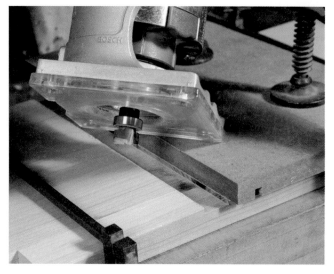

Rout the dadoes for the shelf and divider. The upper dado is through, but the lower one is stopped. Latta clamps an MDF spacer square to the case to ride a short pattern bit against. A piece of scrap secured to the case's front edge prevents any blowout on the workpiece.

movable stop, and flip the boards edge for edge and end for end for the other tails. The rabbet at the back of the case could interfere with this, but there's an easy workaround: a spacer.

To let me flip the stock, I attach a ⅜-in.-thick spacer to the case's front edge. This spacer matches the depth of the rabbet, thereby offsetting the case that amount to set the stage for easy symmetrical tails.

Setup stick ensures accurate measurement between dadoes. With the case dry-fitted, put the rabbeted setup stick between the dadoes (top). This will push out any cup, giving you an accurate measurement (above) for cutting shelves to length.

Cut dovetails on the fixed shelf. The fixed shelf is installed using a stepped dovetail. After using a setup piece to set the correct bit height, Latta routs a dovetail across both ends of the shelf (top). Then he trims away all but the front inch of the dovetail at the scrollsaw (above).

Transfer the tail to the case. With the shelf dry-fitted in the case, Latta uses a sharp knife to outline the tail on the case sides. Make sure the shelf is seated tightly in the dadoes.

Saw and chisel out the waste. Remove most of the waste with angled sawcuts and rough chisel work. Then take light paring cuts to finish the housing.

Dry-fit the dovetails. Lightly tap the shelf into place, driving each end evenly to avoid racking.

Dry-fit the horizontal divider before laying out dadoes for the vertical ones. Instead of measuring to lay out the dadoes, use MDF spacers referenced off the case sides, a more accurate and repeatable method.

Rout the dadoes in the shelf and horizontal divider. Remove the workpieces to rout them. As he did with the previous dadoes, Latta registers a pattern bit off a fence.

At the end, return the blade to 90° to cut the space next to the rabbet, leaving you with straight tabs that will fill the rabbets in the case sides.

Next, rabbet the tails. This will help with registration when you transfer the tail layout to the pin board. Start with the rabbet's shoulder cut. It must be perfectly in line with the dovetail baseline. Rather than risk my actual case parts, I use the scrap that has the tails' baseline scribed onto it to position the rip fence. Rabbet the setup stick that matches the top and bottom too. Finally, lay out and cut the pins, then trim the tabs to length.

Dadoes and dovetails

The fixed shelf and horizontal divider sit in dadoes, which I rout with a ⅝-in. bit and ½-in. bit, respectively. The upper dado runs the width of the case side and has a dovetailed housing in front; the lower dado is stopped (bottom photo, p. 164).

To rout these dadoes, I register a short pattern bit off MDF spacers. This type of bare-bones fence cuts down on errors due to measuring. Using a ruler to lay out the dadoes and then aligning a fence to each line is inviting mistakes and inconsistency. Using a spacer, on the other hand, all but guarantees repeatability. Later, I use different spacers for the dadoes for the vertical dividers.

The fixed shelf is special. It is mounted via a stepped dovetail-and-dado joint. Although it's not difficult, it has certain nuances. Done incorrectly, it can distort the case, causing headaches later on. So just as with the rest of the build, accuracy is key, and setup pieces are the way to get there.

Assemble the case and check for square. Insert the rabbeted setup stick between the

Build from the outside in. Glue the carcase together and check for square. With well-cut dovetails, you won't need clamps unless you have to square up the case. To check, measure opposing corner-to-corner distances. If they're equal, the case is square.

Install and flush the shelf. After cutting the stepped dovetails, rip the shelf just slightly over width and glue it in place. Then carefully plane it flush.

Mark and cut the divider's notch. The horizontal divider fits in a stopped dado and gets notched at the front. To mark for the notch, Latta slides the divider in place and scribes it with a chisel flush to the case.

Add the packer strips. Thin strips glued to the bottom act as runners for the lower drawers, elevating them and preventing contact with the applied bead below. Notch the front packer to match the case dado.

Mark the vertical dividers' lengths before gluing them in.
The horizontal and vertical dividers, still overwide here, get ripped to the same size, so you need to mark only one. Be sure to notch these dividers too.

Glue in the fascia and screw rail. The fascia at the front provides a place to attach the molding; the screw rail at the back lets you mount the cabinet to the wall.

Carefully positioned screws will be concealed.
Screws add extra holding power for the fascia and screw rail. Place them so they'll be hidden by the cabinet's molding.

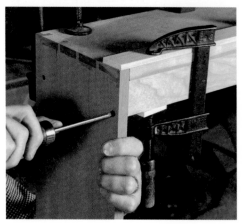

pairs of shelf dadoes to guarantee the case sides are spaced properly for measurement. Each dovetail is ⅜ in. long, so take the distance between the bottoms of the dadoes and add ¾ in. to get the length of the shelf. Cut the shelf to length, leaving it overwide at this point, and cut a setup strip to the same length. To cut the tails, I use a router table with a large dovetail bit buried into a tall zero-clearance fence. The setup strip helps me dial in the router table's settings. You want as wide a tail as possible, and the shoulder-to-shoulder distance should match the dado-to-dado distance on the case.

When the setup is correct, rout a dovetail on each end of the shelf and then crosscut off all but the front inch. Insert the shelf into the dadoes, check for square, and transfer the dovetail to the case. Form the dovetail housing only ½ in. into the case so that when you insert the shelf, it sticks out ½ in. Leaving it proud protects the tails from your hammer blows during test fitting. Rip it close to final width when you're ready to assemble the case.

Before gluing up the case, bore the shelf-pin holes for the movable shelves. I use dividers for layout. Finally, glue up the case, install the shelf, and plane it flush. Notch and install the dividers, put the packer strips in place, and attach the fascia board and screw rail.

Strategic moldings

The cabinet's moldings are fairly simple: two beads and a cove up top, and a single large bead at the bottom. Cutting and installing them correctly, however, takes finesse.

Tablesawing the cove molding is simple but slow. That's because you can take only light passes, raising the blade a slight amount after each cut. Adjust the angle of the auxiliary fence to dial in the shape.

Crown and Beads

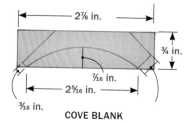

COVE BLANK

2⅞ in.

¾ in.

⁷⁄₁₆ in.

2⁵⁄₁₆ in.

³⁄₁₆ in.

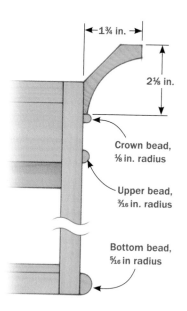

1¾ in.

2⅛ in.

Crown bead,
⅛ in. radius

Upper bead,
³⁄₁₆ in. radius

Bottom bead,
⁵⁄₁₆ in radius

Cove the crown. Ride the workpiece against a fence clamped at an angle. Keep the stock pressed firmly to the table as well. With the blade at 90°, take light passes, raising the blade slightly each time.

Offset Fence

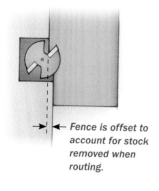

Fence is offset to account for stock removed when routing.

Make an offset fence for routing the beads. Stepping back the infeed side ¹⁄₃₂ in. ensures the board is supported on both sides of the cut.

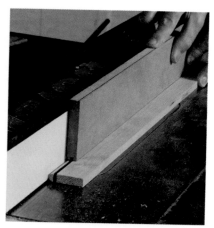

Rout beads on wide stock, then rip them free. The wide blank allows you to work safely, keeping your fingers out of harm's way. Sand the beads before sawing them off.

The trick with the bead moldings is in how you handle them. Since they're too small to be machined safely or well one by one, keep the stock overlong and overwide for as long as you can. Also, because the beading bits trim the entire edge of the board, just like a jointer does, I use an offset fence at the router table. The outfeed side of the fence is proud of the infeed side by ¹⁄₃₂ in. This way, the workpiece is supported on both sides of the cut.

When I hang moldings, I miter, fit, and mount the center piece first. Any tweaking will occur on the side pieces. This way, I'm futzing with fewer miters. Once the miters are tight, I mark and trim the side pieces to length. I make these return cuts last because they're simple straight cuts.

I use spacers again when I am attaching the molding at the top of the case for easy, consistent results. After installing the bead in line with the bottom edge of the fascia board, I lay ¹⁵⁄₁₆-in.-wide spacers right above it. They guarantee the crown bead is parallel to the lower one. Install the coved piece directly above the crown bead. The bead on the bot-

tom of the cabinet is simply flush with the bottom of the case.

Wrap up the case

Three tasks remain before I add finish: adding the backboards, and making the drawers and the doors.

The back consists of ⅜-in.-thick curly maple boards that have their edges beveled and a loose spline between them. These boards are simply nailed in place. Leave about ¹⁄₁₆ in. between the boards to allow for a little movement. The drawers are dovetailed and planed to fit. When I can, I like to use vintage glass in these doors. It adds a lot of subtle character.

I give everything a final sanding and finish the cabinet with General Finishes Arm-R-Seal. Four to five coats with plenty of time to dry in between should do it.

Bigger bead goes on first. The bottom of this bead sits flush with the bottom edge of the fascia board. Start with the front piece, mitering it to the proper length and pinning it in place, before attaching the two side pieces. Adjust the miters only on the side moldings.

TIP Spacers help with the crown bead. By using a pair of plywood spacers ripped to the right width, Latta ensures the two beads are parallel.

Cut the crown in a cradle. The cradle, simply an L of wood, improves indexing and reduces tearout. It also works well for mitering the beads.

Crown molding is flush to crown bead. Brads hold the molding in place. As you did with the beads, miter and attach the front piece of crown before moving to the sides.

Use Vintage Glass for Cabinet Doors

STEVE LATTA

New clear

New antique

You took great care when you selected the wood for your new cabinet, and then you poured yourself into the milling, joinery, and assembly. Now that the divided-light doors are built, what will you do about the glass?

Glass purchased from the hardware store is sterile and lifeless; it takes more away from your piece than it contributes. Vintage glass, by contrast, has a vitality that adds something extra to the finished piece. Old processes of making window glass produced panes with ripples and bubbles and varying thickness, and it is these blemishes that make old glass so vibrant. Old panes reflect and refract light unpredictably, creating glints and shadows that make it a pleasure to open a door. In this chapter, I'll tell you where to get old glass, how to salvage it from window frames, and how to work with it.

In search of old glass

The search for old glass is part of the fun of using it. Antique stores, junk shops, and

Glass forager. Great old glass for your next glazed cabinet is as close as the nearest flea market, antique store, or architectural salvage company.

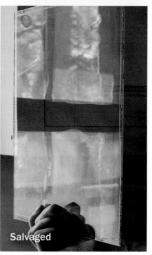

Salvaged

Reflections tell the tale. An outdoor scene reflected in three types of glass shows the difference between a clear new pane, new-made antique-style glass, and vintage glass, with its subtle waves and distortions.

flea markets often have old windows, and I typically pay between $15 and $25 per sash. Architectural salvage companies are another good source and often have a broader selection. Once you're on the lookout, you'll also notice windows on the side of the road waiting for the garbage truck—this may be less predictable, but you can't beat the price. My current favorite source is a local company that installs replacement windows. They had hundreds of old sashes out in the weather, leaning up against their building, and they told me to take whatever I needed, no charge. Nice!

When you're on the prowl for glass, bring along paper towels and glass cleaner so you can see what you're getting. Once you have the panes clean enough to get a reflection, make sure the glass has a nice ripple by looking at it from an angle. Raking light can help reveal the character of the glass as well. Every now and then you'll get some bubbles in the glass. These are simply gorgeous, but much less common than a good ripple.

Liberate the glass (and sacrifice the frame). Latta clips the corners off the sash to remove the joinery. He carefully pries apart the frame and removes the glass. He wears a respirator in case he's dealing with lead-based paint.

Careful cleanup. Using a scrap of low-pile carpet as a cushion, Latta removes the old glazing compound with a razor blade, then thoroughly cleans the glass.

Cut the glass to size. Cutting old glass is no different from cutting new. Latta marks it with a Sharpie and scores it with a glass cutter guided along a straightedge. His Masterforce straightedge (menards.com) has a rubbery strip underneath to keep it from slipping on the glass.

Installation option 1: Solid wood retaining strips. Whether he's using glazing compound or wood strips to secure the glass, Latta starts by tacking the pane in place with a few spots of silicone glass sealant.

Fit four sides, fix three. Latta cuts the miters on all four strips, then tacks all but the bottom piece in place with a brad nailer.

Roughly speaking, the older the glass the better. Most window glass made in the last 60 years or so—called float glass and made by pouring liquid glass onto a bed of molten tin—is perfectly flat, perfectly free of blemishes, and perfectly boring. Prior to that, most window glass was made by first creating a large glass cylinder, closed at both ends. The ends were removed and the remaining sleeve of glass was slit along its length, reheated, flattened, and then cut into panes. Before the 20th century, a blowpipe was typically used to make the cylinder, producing panes that were full of character. The blowpipe technique was supplanted by a mechanized method of pulling a cylinder of glass; the resulting panes were more uniform, but still showed some ripple and irregularities.

Check all the panes in a sash. You don't want to buy a nice old six-light sash and get home to find that one or two of the panes are originals and the rest are recent replacements. Not all replacements are useless, however. In one large, twin-light sash I found, I could tell that both panes were old glass. When I got them out of the frame and cleaned, however, I discovered that one pane was older than the other. One had a brown tint, the other green; they differed in thickness and one had more

Bisect the bottom. To make the strips easier to remove in the future, Latta cuts the bottom strip in half with a thin-kerf razor saw. Then he tacks the two halves in place.

ripple. Still, they were both very desirable, and I used them in the same cabinet.

Occasionally you'll find a pane with good ripple but with some clouding that simply will not come off. I'll sometimes use a clouded pane anyway, if the cabinet I've built has a dark interior; but if it is a light contemporary piece where the blemish might show, I won't.

Retrieve and cut the glass

To harvest the glass from an old window, I first cut the corners off the frames, removing the joinery that holds the window together. Then I gently pull the stiles and rails apart and take the panes out. Once the glass is removed from the frames, clean it before cutting. The old glazing compound usually comes off readily, and I use a razor blade to remove the residue. If the glazing is stubborn and your glass is large enough, you can simply cut the edges off, glazing and all.

To cut the glass, I use a glass cutter and glass running pliers, available at the hardware store for less than $20 each. Old glass cuts like new glass, except that it is a little more fragile and tends to have a greater failure rate. If I need 16 panes for a set of bookcase doors, I'll make sure I have five or six extra panes on hand.

With a Sharpie, mark a couple of points to establish your first cut line. Moisten the cutter wheel with light oil and, using the cutter and a straightedge, score the pane in a single pass. Tap along the underside of the score line with the ball at the end of the cutter. Then use glass pliers to snap off the waste piece. Next, cut a perpendicular edge. Then fit the glass into a corner of the opening to mark the other two edges.

Installation

When the pane is cut to size, tack it in place using tiny dabs of clear silicone. You don't need a whole bead; just a few dabs will hold it securely. Once the silicone sets, you can use either solid wood retaining strips or glazing compound to finish the installation.

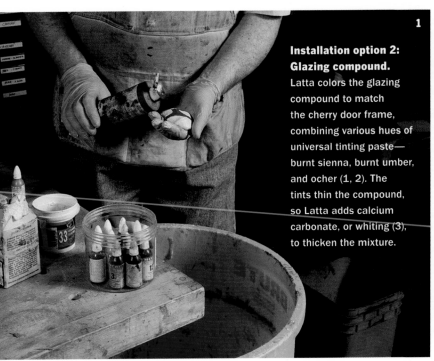

Installation option 2: Glazing compound. Latta colors the glazing compound to match the cherry door frame, combining various hues of universal tinting paste— burnt sienna, burnt umber, and ocher (1, 2). The tints thin the compound, so Latta adds calcium carbonate, or whiting (3), to thicken the mixture.

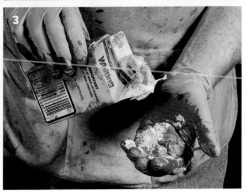

Pressed in place. After kneading the glazing into ropes and pushing it into place with his fingers (right), Latta uses a laminate sample to press it home (far right). He uses a chisel moistened with jojoba oil to produce the final, clean bevel on the glazing (below).

Foolproof Inset Cabinet Doors

STEFAN STRAKA

Whether you're building a piece of furniture or a kitchen's worth of cabinets, there's no substitute for the clean look of inset doors with traditionally mortised butt hinges. Many of us approach our first set of these doors with trepidation, however. You've put a lot of time and effort into the project, and now you have one chance to fit each door with even reveals—the gaps between the door and the face frame.

The challenge with inset doors lies in the way they are boxed in on all sides, allowing your eye to pick up the slightest differences

Rip your shims. Make thin rips on the tablesaw until you get a strip equal in thickness to your desired door reveals, in this case, just under ⅛ in. (The gaps will end up very close to ⅛ in. after you sand the edges of the door.) Then cut the strip to make four shims.

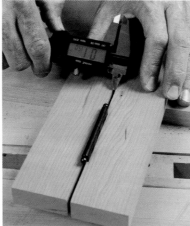

Dial in your hinge-mortising jig. Mortise two test pieces, equal in size to a door stile and a face-frame stile, to test the mortise depth and ensure a precise gap on the hinge side of the door.

Mortise the face frame. Mortising is easier to do on the loose stiles. Once this is done, assemble your face frames.

in the reveals. Things would be easier if you were fitting perfect rectangles into other perfect rectangles, but that often isn't the case with custom cabinetry. Wood moves, face frames shift during glue-up, and uneven clamping pressure can leave doors slightly out of square. Using a butt hinge—with no adjustability—adds another level of difficulty, requiring that you trim and mount your door perfectly the first time.

Most of the door-fitting techniques I learned early on involved some combination of using a large sled on the tablesaw, educated guesswork for shimming the door on the sled, and carefully tuned hand planes. I was never satisfied with the process, and was always looking for a more streamlined and repeatable approach. The method I use now removes the guesswork and the many trips

back and forth from the tablesaw or bench to creep up on the right reveal for each edge. It's faster and relatively foolproof.

I'll take you through the steps for mounting a door with butt hinges. There are two tools at the heart of my approach: a set of digital calipers and a track saw. The calipers help me size the wood shims I use to position the door in the opening and mark its edges, and the track saw makes clean, precise trim cuts at my pencil marks. If you don't own a track saw, I hope this helps convince you of its value. Compact and portable yet extremely accurate, it's often the first tool I recommend to people asking for guidance when setting up shop.

Following the steps here will ensure that all your doors and drawers have consistent reveals around them, giving your cabinetry a very refined look. Another subtle detail I like is that the bottom door rails, which don't get trimmed, end up slightly wider than the top ones.

Dial in your shims and mortises

For cabinets with solid-wood door frames and traditional butt hinges, aim for a ⅛-in. reveal on all sides of the door. This size gap accommodates seasonal wood movement and potential binding, and it suits most drawer slides, which have a bit of play in them. Start with the door sized to fit snug in the opening. To set the reveal, make a set of four shims that are just a hair thinner than your desired gap and make another two shims that are exactly ⅛ in. thick to check your reveals later. You can rip the shims a little fat on the tablesaw and then fine-tune them with a drum sander or rip your shim stock to exact size on the saw, bumping the fence until you have a strip that's just right. To ensure a perfect gap on the hinge side of the door, dial in the depth on your hinge-mortising jig before you start.

Test-fit the doors. After assembling the face frames, build the doors to fit the opening dimensions exactly, and trim them for a snug fit if necessary. Don't worry about tapered gaps here; the fitting process will erase those. Label the top-left corner of the door to help you keep track of its orientation.

Sand the bottom. This is the last time you'll want to remove any material from the bottom edge, so sand it through all but your final grit now.

Trim the top to fit the bottom

To begin, the doors need to be able to slide into their openings, but just barely. If you notice that the doors or face frames are slightly out of square at this point, leaving a tapered gap in one or two spots, rest assured that the ⅛-in. reveals will erase those. The

Mark the top edge. Set the shims at the bottom of the face-frame opening and place the door against them, with its top edge resting against the top of the face frame. Mark the top of the door where it hits the frame and transfer those pencil marks onto the face of the door for trimming.

purpose of this first cut along the top edge is actually to set the gap at the bottom edge, which won't be trimmed at all. You'll trim the top edge again later, to perfect its reveal.

Tune up your track saw. Stick a new splinter guard on the edge of a track saw and trim it with a fresh blade. This will make setup accurate and the saw cut cleanly.

Make a smooth trim cut. For this cut, set up the track saw to just remove the pencil marks. Note the scrap boards (same thickness as the door) placed at the front and back edge. Those keep the track level at both ends of the cut and prevent blowout at the back edge. Set the cutting depth of your saw at least ⅛ in. deeper than the door thickness and make sure that it's at full speed and full depth before you start the cut. For best results, cut all the way across in a single, steady push before retracting the saw.

Hinge side comes next

After each edge is trimmed, it is placed back in the opening and against one pair of shims to align it for marking the next edge, which is done using the other pair of identical shims. Place the door back in the opening against the bottom shims again. If it won't fit, you might have to trim some off one side or the other to correct an error in squareness.

Mark the hinge side. With the door in the opening pressed firmly against the bottom shims and lightly against the strike side (opposite the hinges), place some of the same shim stock against the hinge edge of the face frame and mark the hinge side. Align the shim visually with the edge of the face frame and mark the door along the opposite side of the shim. Mark the top and bottom of the hinge edge with a sharp pencil line.

Trim the hinge edge of the door. This cut is in line with the grain, so you can push the extra support boards a little further away, to keep the track even more level. Try to split the lines with the splinter guard to ensure that you aren't removing too much material.

Time to mortise the door

For mortised butt hinges, the next step is transferring the hinge locations from the face frame to the door and routing the hinge mortises. Make sure you have not adjusted your router since you mortised the face frame. If you have, another test mortise is worth the extra time for a perfect hinge-side gap.

Mark the hinge locations. Sand the hinge side lightly and evenly to remove saw marks. Then place the door back in the opening, firmly against the bottom shims, and slide it against the hinge side. Using a sharp knife, transfer the mortise locations from the face frame to the door.

Rout the door mortises. To locate your router jig accurately on the knife lines, run a sharp pencil down each one to help it stand out.

Square the mortises. After routing, take a few moments to square the corners with a chisel.

Test-fit the hinges. Set each side of each hinge into its mortise, use a self-centering bit to drill a single pilot hole for the center screw, and then attach the hinges temporarily with only the center screws. Set the clutch on your driver to the lowest torque setting to prevent stripping the screwheads or pilot holes.

Check the gap. Use the set of shims milled to the full ⅛-in. thickness to inspect the hung door for even reveals on the hinge side and bottom edge. Misalignment along those edges indicates a problem with your router-jig setup. If the mortises are too shallow, reroute them. If too deep, use brass shim stock to shim out the hinge leaves as needed.

Process for paired doors

There is one situation where you need to adjust the above progression: paired doors. If you simply work all the way around one of the doors first with the usu-al process, you'll

end up removing the bulk of the strike-side material from just one door, leaving little to remove from the adjacent one. This will leave the strike-side stiles at different widths, which could be detectable by eye. To address this, I mark the center of the face-frame opening—top and bottom—and take both doors simultaneously through the hinge-mounting step. Then, keeping an eye on that center line, I trim off just enough of each one so the doors can close. Next, to create a perfect gap between the strike-side stiles, I center my marking shim on the face-frame center line and mark both doors at the same time, top and bottom.

One step for the final edges

For individual doors like the one shown here, with the door mounted, you can now simply mark the strike side of the door and top edges at the same time to finish the process.

Mark the top side and strike side. Use the same shim-marking technique, being very careful to line up the outside of the shim with the inside of the face frame.

Final cuts. Set up your last two cuts just like before, with the edge of the track just splitting the lines and scrap boards arranged to keep the track level and prevent blowout.

One last check. Slip the hinges and ⅛-in. shims into place to check the reveals. You can always take off another sliver if necessary. Now you can sand the last two edges to create the full ⅛-in. reveal.

Contemporary Door and Drawer Pulls

LARISSA HUFF AND ROBERT SPIECE

When we design and make custom furniture, we also design and make the pulls. We often leave pull design until deep into the building process so that we can use the physical piece for inspiration. Making those final details is exciting because they can be what brings the whole piece together—the icing on the cake, if you will.

Our pull designs vary, but one common denominator is batch production. We always need multiple pulls (which are typically made with tiny parts) and we want making them to be a safe, efficient process that yields consistent results. For us, that means designing good procedures and building good jigs. We'll explain how we made these particular splined and mitered pulls, but the thinking behind the jigs and processes can be applied to other designs.

Marking and cutting the miters

We made the pulls in two sizes, shorter for doors and longer for drawers. To create a continuous grain match, we cut the three parts for each pull from a single blank. After milling all the blanks, we accurately laid out the parts for one short pull on a short blank and one long pull on a long blank. The blanks for the rest of the pulls were just quickly marked with chalk to indicate the direction of the miters. Using a different color marker for each blank, we also drew an offset line

Grain Wraps Around Mitered Pulls

To make continuous-grain pulls, cut the three parts for each pull from a single blank. Blanks for door pulls are ½ in. by ⅞ in. by 11¼ in. For drawer pulls, blanks are ½ in. by ⅞ in. by 13⅝ in.

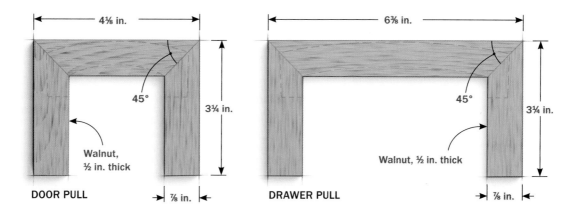

DOOR PULL

4⅛ in.

45°

3¼ in.

Walnut, ½ in. thick

⅞ in.

DRAWER PULL

6⅜ in.

45°

3¼ in.

Walnut, ½ in. thick

⅞ in.

A sled to miter the parts. A tablesaw sled with a 45° fence, a stop block, spacers, and a toggle clamp make cutting the miters on small parts accurate, repeatable, and safe.

First leg first. To cut the first leg, place the longest spacer against the fence and the stop block. Then slide the blank up to the spacer and engage the toggle clamp. The chalk layout lines remind you which way the miters go. After cutting the leg miter, turn the blank over to cut the first miter for the pull's crosspiece, trimming as little off the end as possible.

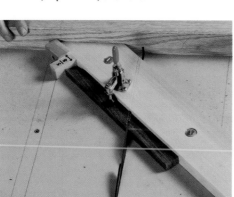

Cut the crosspiece. After cutting the first miter on the crosspiece, flip the blank again, insert the short spacer, and make the second miter cut on the crosspiece.

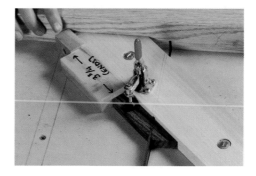

Second leg finishes up the miter cuts. With the leg spacer back in place, cut the final leg miter.

Template Routing Jig

Pull

Hold down,
½ in. thick by 1 in.
wide by 2 in. long

Adjustable stop,
½ in. thick by ⅞ in.
wide by 5 in. long

Back stop, ½ in.
thick by 2½ in.
wide by 11 in. long

Base, plywood,
½ in. thick by 5 in.
wide by 14 in. long

Tackle the inside curve. Before gluing up the pull, you need to cut and finish the inside curve on the crosspiece. To do so make a simple fixture. On the bandsaw, cut the curve of the pull into a piece of plywood. Add stops and a hold down to keep the blank in place during routing.

Shape and sand the inside curve. With the blank in the jig, take multiple shallow passes with a bearing-guided straight bit to cut the curve. You can easily sand the inside curve with a sanding drum on the drill press.

along the outer facing edge of the blank to keep track of the continuous grain after the parts had been cut.

To miter the tiny parts safely, we made a small sled with an angled fence and a toggle clamp (photos, p. 187). We fixed a stop block to the fence 6 in. to the right of the line of cut. Then we made spacer blocks that register against the fixed stop to control the length of the various parts being mitered. We used the accurately laid-out blanks to determine the correct length for the different spacers. Our spacer block for the legs of both pulls was 3¾ in., but you could vary this based on your sled. Our spacer block for the longer pull's crosspiece was ⅝ in., and for the shorter pull's crosspiece it was 2¾ in. Once the spacers are made, you can cut all the miters.

Shaping the inside curves

Before the miters are glued together, you'll shape the inside curve of the crosspieces. A template routing jig helps shape the small pieces safely. We made one for the shorter pulls and another one for the longer pulls.

After sawing and smoothing the desired curve in the edge of a piece of ½-in. plywood, mount a back stop, two adjustable end stops, and a hold-down. Use a router table with a pattern bit to ride the template and copy the curve into the inside edge of the pull. Take several light passes, removing slightly more material with each pass until the bearing of the bit rides along the template. After routing, clean up any machine or burn marks with a quick stop at the spindle sander or by hand sanding.

Glue up and reinforce the miters

To glue the miters we use the quick, effective rub joint. On a clean, flat surface, apply glue and slide the mating miters against each other until the two tack together. Apply

Fine-tune the joint. Prior to glue-up, Huff uses a handplane on a shooting board to clean up the miters.

Rub joint gets the job done. Use a dab of glue and rub the joints back and forth against each other until the glue grabs. Hold the joint firmly in place for about 30 seconds and leave the pulls to dry overnight.

Cut the legs to length. After glue-up, use another simple jig to hold the pull in place while cutting the legs to length on the tablesaw.

End run around end grain. Because screws into end grain can weaken over time, add threaded inserts to the legs. Bore holes for them on the drill press. Use a fence, a stop block, and a toggle clamp to keep the piece firmly against the fence. But don't glue the inserts in place yet.

finger pressure for half a minute and let them dry overnight.

Then cut the legs to length on the tablesaw. To do it safely, we use a simple sliding jig with a fence and a toggle clamp. Next drill holes into the ends of the legs. Mounting pulls by screwing into end grain is not a plan for longevity, so we add threaded inserts, and these holes accept them.

To strengthen the tiny miter joints, we use shopmade keys made from the same wood as the pulls. To cut slots for the keys, we made a jig that straddles the tablesaw's rip fence and cradles the pull at 45°. Once we've cut the slots, we use a caliper to measure the width of the kerf, and then rip key stock at the tablesaw to fit the kerf. Rip several long strips to thickness and hand-cut or bandsaw the keys to length. Apply glue to the slot and the

key. Press the key into place, ensuring it seats fully, and leave it to dry.

Shaping and finishing touches

We trace a template to establish the outside shape of the pull. Then we cut the shape at the bandsaw and refine it on a disk sander. The cross-grain disk sander scratches are removed on the sanding belt.

With a ⅛-in.-radius bit at the router table, round over all the edges. Sand the pull flat by rubbing it on 180-grit sandpaper on a flat surface. Touch up the edges with 180-grit to remove tearout from the router.

To further refine the shape and give the pull a nice, soft quality, we finish up those hard-to-reach edges with a flap sander in the drill press. This sanding tool gives the pull

Kerf the pulls and install the keys. Two final construction details are adding the keys to the miters and shaping the outside of the pulls. With an over-the-fence sled cradling the pull at 45°, cut a kerf (with a thin-kerf rip blade) in the center of the miters and glue in the keys. The keys should be longer and wider than the key slot to make gluing them in easier.

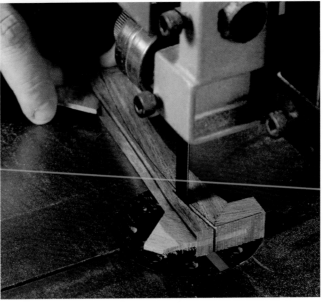

The outer shape. Use a template to trace the final shape on all the pulls. Then carefully cut that shape out on the bandsaw.

Smooth the sawmarks. After bandsawing the outside shape of the pulls, sand them to a finished surface. A stationary belt sander refines the shape and removes machine marks. It's followed by a flap sander on the drill press.

Round it over. With a ⅛-in. roundover bit at the router table, round all the edges of the pull, except the bottom of the legs. Then hand-sand to remove any machine marks.

Pop the grain with finish. Huff and Spiece start with boiled linseed oil to bring out the grain of the wood, and then they topcoat with spray lacquer from a can.

a wonderfully tactile feel. Be sure to wear gloves as it is not such a lovely, tactile feel on your bare hand.

Finishing up

Walnut really comes to life with a splash of boiled linseed oil. The pulls are liberally wiped with oil, then wiped clean and left to dry for five days. We topcoat them with spray lacquer. Apply three coats, buffing with 0000 steel wool in between.

Threaded inserts are the final step. Use 5-minute epoxy to secure the inserts. The insert has a shoulder, and a barbed shaft that fits a ¼-in.-dia. hole (stafast.com, No. TS083207).

Build a Custom Rollout Cabinet

PAUL JOHNSON

W hen designing a kitchen remodel for some of my favorite clients, we wanted to eliminate an awkward pinch point created by an existing peninsula without losing the counter space. The kitchen is just narrow enough that a dedicated island wouldn't work, but big enough that we wanted to somehow utilize the full space. We decided on a small rollout cabinet that could easily move around to wherever the homeowners would be working in the kitchen. We wanted to integrate it seamlessly with the rest of the cabinetry, but without it being fussy to take out or put in.

I wanted the cart to look like the rest of the cabinetry, which meant keeping the reveal around it as small as possible—not an easy task considering the 100-year-old out-of-level floor it would be rolling on. I had the tile guys do their best to flatten the old floor when they put in the new tile, but I also decided to build the cabinet carcase separately, fit it into place, and then attach the face frame so I could ensure a consistent gap all the way around. I tacked the face frame into place with glue and a few brads, and then fully attached it with pocket screws.

To allow for the cart to be pushed into place easily, but also to center itself without adjustment, I built housing that tapers toward the back and then straightens out. The front of the housing is 1 in. wider than the width of the cabinet but tapers back to a section that is only 1/16 in. wider than the cabinet. The face frame overhangs the sides of the cabinet by 1/4 in. to hide the additional room at the front. I wanted to leave ample room for adjustment and to hide any inconsistencies between the rolling cabinet and the fixed cabinet it fits between, so I settled on a 1/4-in. gap. As it turns out, everything worked so well that I think I could have gotten away with a 1/8-in. gap instead.

I had originally envisioned a wider cabinet opening with high-density plastic rails or guides of some sort, but I didn't want anything to mar the paint on the rollout cabinet over time, so I settled on lining the opening with the same prefinished maple plywood I use for cabinet

Custom Rollout Cabinet

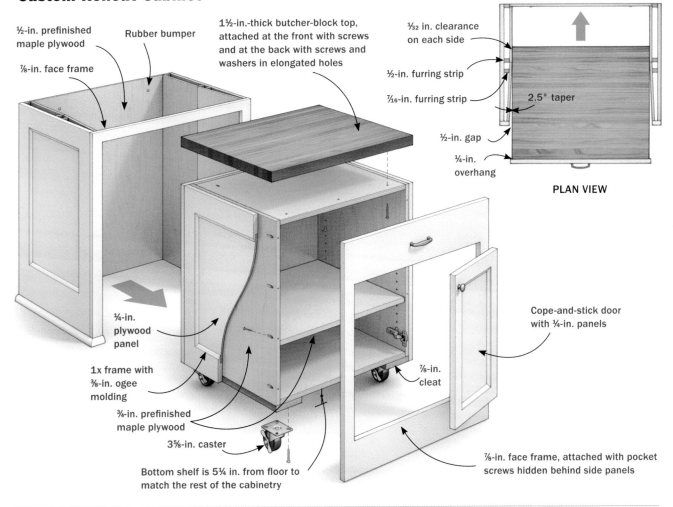

½-in. prefinished maple plywood

Rubber bumper

⅞-in. face frame

1½-in.-thick butcher-block top, attached at the front with screws and at the back with screws and washers in elongated holes

1/32 in. clearance on each side

½-in. furring strip

7/16-in. furring strip

2.5° taper

½-in. gap

¼-in. overhang

PLAN VIEW

Cope-and-stick door with ¼-in. panels

¼-in. plywood panel

1x frame with ⅜-in. ogee molding

¾-in. prefinished maple plywood

3⅝-in. caster

Bottom shelf is 5¼ in. from floor to match the rest of the cabinetry

⅞-in. cleat

⅞-in. face frame, attached with pocket screws hidden behind side panels

construction. The finish is slick and rock solid, so it should wear well over time, and it allows the cart to slide in and out effortlessly.

We're lucky to have a great store in town that specializes in casters (johnwnegus.com), so before I started construction, I went there to get help figuring out the best casters to use. We settled on medium-duty swiveling and locking casters that roll easily but have enough resistance that the cart won't roll away on its own. I installed the casters far enough inside the cabinet's footprint that they don't extend past the sides of the cabinet when swiveling.

When the homeowners chose butcher block for the top, I knew that because wood moves, I'd have to be thoughtful about how to attach it. I chose to screw it to the cabinet from below. In the front, I screwed it tight; in the back, I routed slotted holes to allow the wood top to move. This way, any movement will be toward the back and won't create a gap between the top and the face frame where crumbs and debris could potentially collect.

The result is a fully functional, movable island that rolls wherever the owners need, doesn't take up any room in a somewhat narrow space, and integrates seamlessly into the cabinetry.

The Practical Details of Kitchen Islands

MATTHEW MILLHAM

Oh, the kitchen island. Almost everybody seems to want one, and for good reason. With the kitchen and entertaining spaces of homes increasingly melding together, islands serve numerous purposes. They're transitional areas, where one side may pull double duty as a homework desk and dining counter. They help define the area between the kitchen and the space beyond. They're social gathering places that allow the cook to interact with family and guests. But ultimately, they're part of the kitchen, and they need to play nice with it. Before even thinking about aesthetics, it's important to nail down the practical details. Above all, an island should add functionality and efficiency to a kitchen, not hamper them. Here are some guidelines and ideas to help you get the most out of your kitchen island and get the thumbs-up from code-enforcement officers.

Working dimensions

An oversize, undersize, or misplaced island can wreak havoc on kitchen efficiency, causing more problems than it solves. Keep these basic principles in mind when sizing and placing a kitchen island.

CLEARANCES DETERMINE AVAILABLE SPACE

Even a small island has big space requirements. The National Kitchen and Bath Association (NKBA) recommends that work aisles be at least 42 in. wide for one cook and at least 48 in. wide for two or more cooks. Walkways that pass around the island should be at least 36 in. wide. If the island has a seating area, and no traffic passes behind the seated diners, the recommended minimum space from the edge of the counter to an adjacent wall or obstruction is 32 in. For room to shuffle behind seating, increase the distance to 36 in. For walking room, bump it up to 44 in. Practically, what does that mean? Say you have a 3-ft. by 5-ft. island. For a rough estimate, figure 42 in. all around. The actual space required to accommodate this modest island is 120 sq. ft. These are just guidelines, though, not code requirements, and they're considering the "average" user. Families or cooks that are on the petite side can easily get away with narrower work aisles.

THE WORK TRIANGLE STILL WORKS

The work triangle has been the backbone of efficient kitchen design for more than half a century, and it revolves around the three primary work centers—the sink, the range, and the refrigerator. These elements are typically arranged in a triangle, with no leg less than 4 ft. long and none longer than 9 ft. Nothing should get in the way of any leg of the work triangle—including an island. Think about how you move through the kitchen and how many times things will need to be moved to go from storage to prep to cooking. Keeping the work triangle free of obstructions reduces unnecessary moves. Incorporating a work center or two into the island can keep it from becoming an obstacle to efficiency. If it obstructs workflow, reconsider the size, shape, and placement of the island, or whether you should have one at all.

USABLE SPACE

There is no ideal size for an island; sizing tends to come down to the space available, how the island fits into the space, and the budget. But there are some guidelines. The entire work surface should be reachable from the work aisles, and the entire island surface should be reachable so it can be cleaned easily. Going wider than about 5 ft. can leave items and debris stranded in the middle. Anything narrower than the depth of standard cabinets (24 in.) won't accommodate sinks, cooktops, or dishwashers, nor will it be very useful for food prep. There is no maximum length for an island, but long islands can be a bear to walk around. Rather than expanding an island to accommodate additional appliances and features, consider breaking it into two. If clearances permit, consider different island shapes—such as an ell—which can result in a bigger island with shorter distances between points.

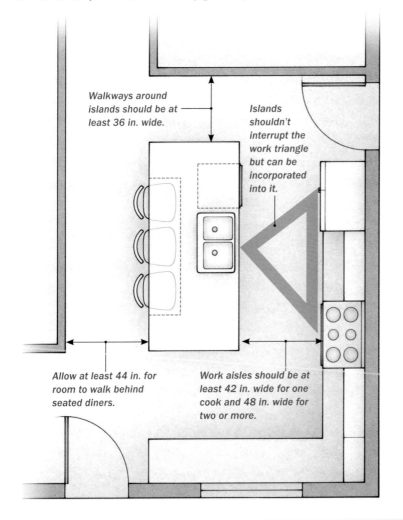

Walkways around islands should be at least 36 in. wide.

Islands shouldn't interrupt the work triangle but can be incorporated into it.

Allow at least 44 in. for room to walk behind seated diners.

Work aisles should be at least 42 in. wide for one cook and 48 in. wide for two or more.

Counter arguments

Islands are the Swiss Army knife of the kitchen, but that doesn't mean the counter should be packed with features and gadgets. A multifunctional counter is one that can be used for many different tasks. Appliances and fixtures quickly eat up counter space and can reduce the overall utility of smaller islands.

HEIGHT MATTERS

An island's primary work surface should be the same height as other counters in the kitchen—around 36 in.—to facilitate easy movement between counters. Beyond that, the choice between a flat or multilevel island comes down to preferences and how it will be used. A flat island—the most common type in new homes and kitchen remodels—is the easiest to clean, lends an open feel, and has a lot to offer in terms of versatility. The entire surface of a flat island can be used for food prep or other tasks while still accommodating a seating area. Varying counter heights has perks, too. A higher portion at the back is a good way to hide the mess of food preparation from guests, and it provides space to put switches and required electrical outlets. For bakers, a lower counter—around 30 in. to 32 in.—is useful for kneading or rolling dough. But varying counter heights can also be limiting. A higher dining counter at the back of the island, for example, limits that portion to a specific use: eating. A raised counter also tends to wall the kitchen off from the space outside, especially if there's a range hood dangling over the top.

APPLIANCES

The number of appliances available for kitchen islands is constantly growing—everything from wine fridges and ice makers to refrigerator and freezer drawers, as well as the trusty old dishwasher and cooking appliances. Only things the cook needs ready access to should be on the working side of the island, so put any extras on the end, the back side, or somewhere else in the kitchen. If the cleanup sink is in the island, put the dishwasher next to it.

FIXTURES AND LANDING AREAS

Just as varying counter heights can limit the use of island space, the same can be said of fixtures and appliances that take up counter space. If the island will have a sink, range, or cooktop, keep the work triangle in mind when deciding where to put them. If space for an island is limited, leave sinks and cooktops off (or pick the one that's most used) to maintain its multifunctionality. For example, if the cook spends more time preparing food for cooking than cooking it, put the sink in the island to maximize his or her interaction with guests and the home. If the island is going to be the main prep area, place appliances and fixtures in a way that maximizes prep space.

The NKBA recommends a minimum 36-in.-wide by 24-in.-deep counter space immediately next to a sink for the primary prep area, but this is too small for anything more than basic meals. To maximize island prep space, consider put-ting a secondary sink dedicated to food prep near one end of the island, leaving a wide open space next to it. Since prep sinks aren't used for washing up, there's little need for landing space on both sides as there is with a primary sink, where 24 in. on one side and 18 in. on the other is recommended. If the island includes a cooktop or range, the ideal place for the prep area is between it and the prep sink to minimize movement and the possibility of spillage.

For cooking surfaces, the NKBA recommends a 12-in. landing area on one side and 15 in. on the other. If the island is flat, include at least 9 in. of clear space behind the cooking surface for safety. Include landing areas above microwaves, refrigerator drawers, and warmers to place items as they're removed from the appliances. These landing areas can be shared with other landing areas or prep spaces.

SEATING

Seating at an island requires an overhang, and the size of the overhang can vary based on the height of the counter. The higher the counter, the less knee space required, since diners' legs dangle at a steeper angle the higher they sit. The NKBA recommends an 18-in. overhang for 30-in.-high counters, 15-in. overhangs for 36-in.-high counters, and 12-in. overhangs for 42-in.-high counters. Overhangs often require legs, brackets, or other means of support, especially if they're big. If space is tight, raising the dining counter can gain back some inches on the overall width of an island, albeit at the expense of workspace. Dining counters should be at least 18 in. deep, and diners should have at least 2 ft. of counter space per seat to eat comfortably.

Under the counter

This is where the island-as-Swiss-Army-knife analogy is most apt. Limiting or eliminating amenities from island counters frees up space under the counter for additional appliances and storage, which, used wisely, can allow the island to truly serve as a transitional space between the kitchen and beyond.

ELECTRICAL

Code typically requires electrical receptacles on islands and usually allows them to be placed in the countertop (pop-ups), in backsplashes above the counter (in multilevel islands), or in the faces of cabinetry below the counter (where they can be hidden behind false panels). All receptacles serving kitchen counters require ground-fault circuit interrupter (GFCI) protection. By code, the counter can't overhang cabinet-mounted receptacles by more than 6 in., and receptacles can't be more than 12 in. below the counter surface. Flat islands with nothing installed in the counter often need only one receptacle for the entire island, though local codes may require more.

When a sink, range, or cooktop is installed in an island, the spaces on either side of it are considered separate counters unless the counter extends at least 12 in. behind the sink or appliance. Any island countertop space with a long dimension of 24 in. or more, and a short dimension of 12 in. or more, requires its own receptacle.

If you want to avoid the receptacle requirement altogether, consider a large rolling cart or worktable that isn't fastened to the floor.

PLUMBING

Plumbing traps are designed to hold water to prevent sewer gases from backing up into the home. Without proper venting, water gets siphoned out of the traps and sewer gases get in. Vent pipes typically run up through the walls and penetrate the roof. Because of an island's location, venting can be difficult, and there are generally two approved ways to do it. Of the two, the one most likely to provide years of trouble-free service is a bow vent, or "Chicago loop." Bow vents take up considerable cabinet space, require accessible cleanouts, and need to connect with a standard vent stack or stack vent. The other option is an air-admittance valve (AAV), which is much easier to plan for and install. This device opens under negative pressure to allow air into the drain system and closes by gravity once the sink is drained. AAVs are installed just downstream of the trap and at least 4 in. above the horizontal drainpipe that runs out of the trap.

Dishwasher connections vary by local code. Some allow for a "high loop," where the drain line runs from the dishwasher up to the bottom of the counter and back down to the drain system. Others require an "air gap" fixture, which usually gets installed on the sink. In either case, the discharge end of the drain line connects to the sink drain, either to a special fitting located above the trap, or to an inlet on a food disposal.

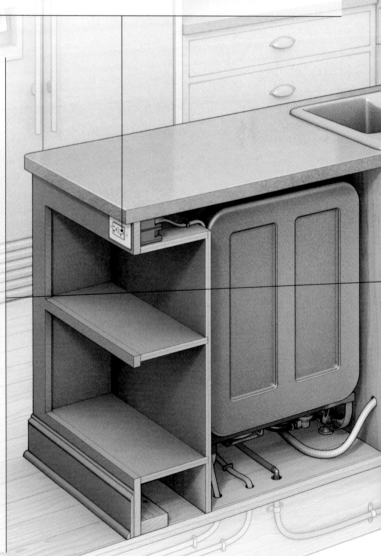

VENTING

Dedicated ventilation for ranges and cooktops isn't always code-required, but when it is installed, it has to follow code. Range hoods must be at least 24 in. above cooking surfaces, and manufacturers' installation specifications and instructions must be followed to pass muster with the code inspector and be covered by the warranty. Ducted range hoods mounted over the cooktop are the most effective option, but island hoods typically have to be larger—extending beyond the footprint of the cooktop—and have more powerful fans than similar wall-mounted hoods to be effective. They can also interfere with sightlines, and models for islands are more expensive than their wall-mounted kin. Ceiling-mounted vent units, which work with standard-height ceilings, or downdraft vents, which mount next to or behind the cooking appliance, won't interfere with sightlines but are generally less effective than overhead hoods. By code, vents that exhaust more than 400 cu. ft. of air per minute require makeup air at a rate equal to the exhaust rate.

Hoods handle odors. Expect to pay more, and to need more makeup air, for an island range hood.

STORAGE

The island should include storage for items that will be used at it, preferably within reach of where they're needed. For example, a drawer of cooking utensils is ideally placed next to the cooktop. Drawers, pullout shelving, and rollout trays generally make it easier to access items than standard shelves do. Open shelving can provide an open and airy feel to an island, but it requires more upkeep than behind-door and drawer options, both in terms of dusting and arrangement. Consider limiting open shelving to cookbooks and easy-to-clean decorative pieces. Make sure cabinet doors and drawers don't interfere with doors and drawers across the work aisle. If your island will have appliance garages for mixers or other items, include electrical connections in the garages for these devices.

ANCHORAGE

Islands are most often anchored with 2x cleats attached to the flooring beneath them. If possible, attach the cleats with long deck screws to the joists below. If the cleats can't be attached to the joists, use construction adhesive and shorter screws to penetrate into the subfloor. Then screw through the bottom of the island's cabinetry and into the cleats to hold it fast.

Multipurpose Kitchen Islands

PAUL DEGROOT

Whether they are planning a kitchen for a new home or remodeling their existing kitchen, most of my clients ask for an island as soon as we start to talk about their project. And most of them describe a workhorse that is handy, functional, durable, and beautiful. They want an island that can support food prep, cooking, cleanup, casual meals, and socializing, as well as doing homework and making crafts. In my experience, however, the first item on a client's island wish list is seating. Here are some tips for designing a multipurpose kitchen island that offers comfortable seating for family and friends.

Start with the seating

Everyone wants a place for the kids to eat breakfast and for friends to sip wine and nibble on appetizers. Island seating can usurp the kitchen table and save valuable floor space. In this way, incorporating seating is one of the first drivers of the design.

If regular chairs are to be used, then part of the island will need to drop down to table height: 29 in. to 30 in. Most folks prefer stools, though. There are stools that fit comfortably under a standard 36-in. countertop, and there are taller stools designed for counters elevated 6 in. to 8 in. above the rest of the island. I prefer the 36-in. countertop. It maximizes the utility of the worksurface, and the shorter stools are easy to use for

young and old alike. There are reasons for an island to have more than one level—hiding a messy counter, for example—but in most cases, a simple single-level counter is all that's needed.

I aim to use the island as a traffic cop. Placed well, it keeps those hanging out in the kitchen from getting in the cook's way. Accordingly, I place seating on the nonkitchen side, closest to the adjacent living or dining room. Sometimes stools are needed on the ends, too, for extra guests or as a place to prepare food while sitting down.

What happens on the working side of the island is dictated primarily by the rest of the kitchen layout. If the sink is by a window, then I consider placing the cooktop and/or the oven in the island. Smaller kitchens with limited wall space are good candidates for this. Cooking at the island frees up more upper-cabinet storage on perimeter walls. Meanwhile, the chef gets a commanding view of the family room and guests.

I've designed a few kitchens with the main sink and the dishwasher located in the island. I think the scarcity of this setup is because folks don't want dirty dishes, pots, and pans in plain view; they don't want raised bar tops to hide the clutter; and they prefer upper cabinets nearby when unloading the dishwasher. However, a secondary sink in the island can add another level of convenience to the kitchen.

Avoid the squeeze

The most common mistakes happen when the kitchen is too small to fit a useful island. The aisles around the island become cramped, and the island itself offers minimal function. Avoid these five common blunders, and you're on your way to designing a smarter island.

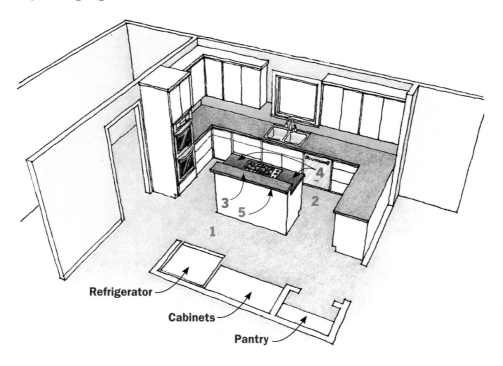

Refrigerator

Cabinets

Pantry

1 The island isolates the sink and the cooktop from the refrigerator.

2 The aisles are too narrow. Two people cannot pass in the aisles, and appliance doors completely stop traffic.

3 The raised counter is too narrow to be useful for eating or for other activities such as doing homework.

4 There is too little counter space on either side of the cooktop.

5 The overhang is inadequate for seating.

Get the size right

I've seen lots of islands tiny enough for me to question their utility. They were plopped into the middle of small kitchens, their owners desperate for more counter space. A common result of this is that the island blocks the normal traffic flow between the sink, the refrigerator, and the cooktop. On the other hand, I've seen islands that were so large that I couldn't reach the middle of them. I try to find the sweet spot for island size. Perhaps more important than size, however, is the amount of space around the island; therefore, I plan aisle widths before island size.

With space comes function

A kitchen is ideally suited for a multipurpose island when all of the cooking and cleaning zones, as well as the appliances, can be located on the inside. The outside then becomes a comfortable place for meals, socializing, and more. Here's why this island works.

OUTSIDE

1 The aisle widths are ample, especially near appliances.

2 The length and the overhang are sufficient for comfortable seating.

3 Extra counter space is available for loading and unloading the refrigerator.

4 A secondary prep sink offers a greater level of function to the kitchen.

5 End shelves display items and cookbooks.

6 Furniturelike legs add style.

INSIDE

7 Drawers make items easier to find.

8 A recessed toe kick on all sides makes it comfortable to stand at the island and hides scuffs.

9 The paint color and counter material add contrast and style.

10 The large, one-level worksurface is more useful for multiple tasks than a multilevel island.

11 Electrical outlets at each end are a code requirement.

12 A drawer-style microwave below the counter is safe for people of all ages to use.

13 Pull-out trash and recycle bins, or vertical dividers for sheet pans or cutting boards, are another smart use of below-counter cabinets.

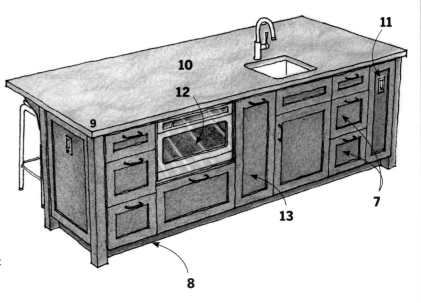

Whenever possible, I give 42 in. to 48 in. to an aisle where an oven door or dishwasher door opens into it. This provides room for a person to maneuver past the door when it's down (a typical dishwasher door can block 26 in. of the aisle). When no door is open, a 48-in.-wide clearance allows two people to walk past each other comfortably. Obviously, there are times when aisles cannot be quite so wide. In such cases, 36 in. should be the minimum clearance, with careful placement of appliances to minimize bottlenecks.

Remember that extra room is needed at the oven door. Removing hot dishes from the oven is difficult and dangerous when a narrow aisle forces you to stand to the side.

Aisles by refrigerators need plenty of space, too; in a busy household, the refrigerator sees a lot of traffic. Consider a 36-in.-wide aisle the minimum; you may want to hold to this size if the island is the nearest countertop to the fridge. Otherwise, use 42 in. to 48 in., especially when your family's main path in and out of the kitchen is via the fridge aisle.

I think any width over 60 in. is excessive for an aisle and an indication that perhaps the kitchen is oversize to start with. I can imagine when such generosity might be warranted—next to a wide exterior door, for example—but day to day, do you really want to turn around from the sink and take four steps or more to get to the island?

The island's length usually is set by the number of stools that are desired. Allowing 24 in. per stool, an island for four ends up being at least 8 ft. long. When room is limited, moving one stool to an end allows you to shorten the length. If you have less than 6 ft. for the length, though, consider a more square shape with stools on three sides.

The recessed area for stools needs to be deep enough to keep shoes from scuffing the cabinetry. I use 18 in. as a minimum, but I prefer 24 in. (Be sure to provide structural support for overhanging countertops.) Couple this dimension with a standard cabinet depth on the working side, and the narrow island dimension ends up being in the 48-in. range. For bigger kitchens, this dimension might approach 60 in., which is the width limit of many countertop slab materials.

Add some style

Regardless of size, islands are an opportunity to add some style to a kitchen. You can use an island to bring contrast to the kitchen's aesthetic, perhaps with a paint color on the cabinets or a counter material that differs from what is used in the rest of the kitchen. A butcher-block countertop looks great as a departure from swaths of shiny stone used to top the main cabinets. The same goes for concrete and soapstone; their matte finishes and natural hues make them irresistibly touchable. Island ends can feature display shelves, furniturelike legs, or a countertop waterfall to enhance the kitchen's style. Lighting above the island is necessary and represents another opportunity to dress up the kitchen. My clients routinely want pendant lights hanging over their islands, not recessed lights. Whether contemporary, traditional or in between, these lights provide a spot of visual punch.

Bathroom Vanities

MARIANNE CUSATO

A well-detailed bathroom vanity is an efficient and elegant piece of furniture in your bathroom, while a poorly detailed vanity is a frustrating eyesore that contributes to marital strife.

The following set of tips can be applied to all styles of cabinetry. The goal of these suggestions is to help you both when building a custom design, as well as selecting a stock product off the shelf.

Vanity size and configuration

DOUBLE-SINK VANITIES

A double-sink vanity is ideally no less than 72 in. wide. They are commercially available starting at 60 in., but before installing the smaller size, it's worth considering the homeowner's pattern of use. Will more than one person be in the bathroom at the same time of day? If not, and if you have limited space, it may be preferable to install a single sink. This leaves more counter space and allows for more drawers for storage. One variation to consider is using a single larger sink with two faucets. This gives the best of both worlds—a little more counter space as well as the ability for two people to use the sink at the same time.

A typical counter height is 36 in., but increasingly we are seeing bathroom vanities installed at 38 in. to make it a little easier to wash your face.

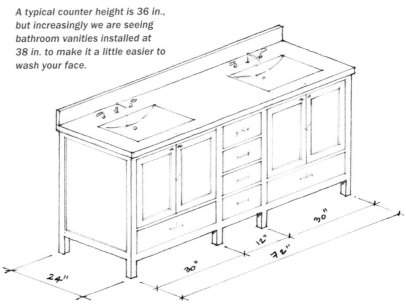

MICRO VANITIES

In urban apartments and smaller homes where every square inch is at a premium, look for a thinner vanity that projects from the wall 18 in. rather than the full 24 in.

SINGLE-SINK VANITIES

A good target dimension for a single vanity is 36 in. This gives enough space for storage and a clear counter. If you are installing in a corner, you can offset the sink to one side to maximize storage. If the vanity is centered in a space, it may look better to center the sink, but this will reduce storage. See p. 208 for notes about corner installations.

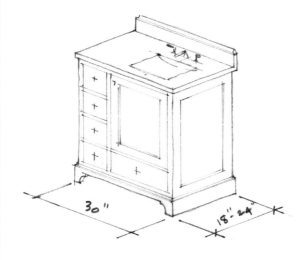

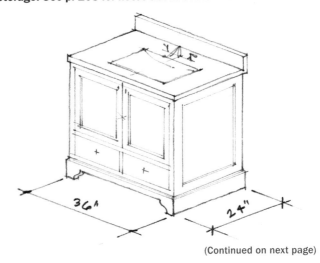

(Continued on next page)

Vanity size and configuration

(Continued from previous page)

CORNER VANITIES

Many, if not most, vanities are located in the corner of a room. This introduces a design dilemma, as most stock vanities are built to be freestanding. If you are unable to purchase a vanity designed to fit into a corner, the next option is to set the vanity four or more inches from the corner; this allows the vanity to be freestanding and, most importantly, allows you to clean between the vanity and the wall easily. Another option is to engage the vanity to the wall. In this case, caulk the joint where the counter meets

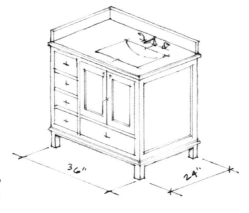

the wall, and also add a thin filler piece to conceal the gap between the wall and the side of the cabinet. Avoid setting the vanity counter less than an inch away from the wall or engaged to the wall without covering the crack. This leaves a space that attracts moisture, dust, and debris and is nearly impossible to clean.

MEGA VANITIES

For larger vanities over 96 in., give or take, consider stepping the cabinetry forward at the sinks to modulate the size of the vanity, making it look more like furniture.

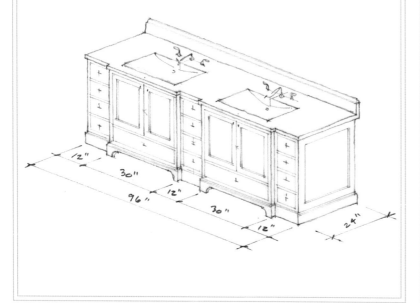

Maximizing storage

Storage and efficiency are essential in a vanity, yet the default design for most vanities includes a fixed panel in front of the sink where the depth of the bowl blocks the path for a drawer. Rather than forfeiting this space, an alternative option is to run a drawer along the bottom of the vanity, then place the cabinet doors above the drawer. You will still have room for the toilet brush and a small trash can.

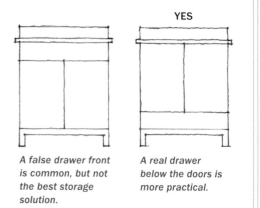

A false drawer front is common, but not the best storage solution.

A real drawer below the doors is more practical.

Toe kicks and feet

Dress the vanity up with feet and legs in front of the toe kick. This makes the vanity feel more like furniture, rather than built-in cabinetry. Profiles include a simple quarter-round cutout or more elaborate cyma-reversa profiles.

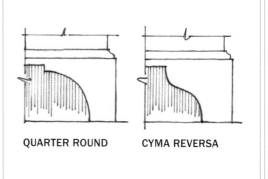

QUARTER ROUND   CYMA REVERSA

Replace Your Vanity

TYLER GRACE

My business specializes in interior renovations, so I'm no stranger to gutting an old bathroom and building it from the studs and subfloor back to a fresh finished space. But in many cases, all that's needed is a facelift to bring the aesthetics into the current decade. Typically, such jobs involve new flooring, trim, plumbing fixtures, lighting, and the cherry on top of the updated finishes: a new vanity.

At its core, the workflow for replacing a vanity is pretty straightforward—turn off and disconnect the plumbing, yank the old vanity out, put the new vanity in, and reconnect the plumbing—but the devil is in the details. If you want the work to look and function at a professional level, there are some subtle steps to the process. You have to know the tricks for removing the old vanity without causing unintended damage, and how to fit the new one without relying heavily on shims and caulk. Moreover, some cautionary knowledge about the plumbing will go a long way toward ensuring that you won't need to make multiple trips to the store for plumbing parts, and that leaks won't ruin all your hard work.

Methodical demo

Removing the old vanity is straightforward work, but these tips on sequencing and site protection will ensure that the task goes smoothly and doesn't risk damaging the rest of the room. First and foremost, before

Plan on spillage. There will be water in the faucet supply lines and a slug of dirty water sitting in the drain trap. Keep things dry by setting a bucket on top of a towel.

Plug the drain pipe. After removing the sink trap, use a rag or a reusable drain plug to block sewer gases from wafting into the room.

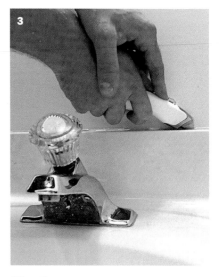

Slice the seams. To minimize drywall damage, cut the caulk around the cabinet and countertop with a sharp utility knife.

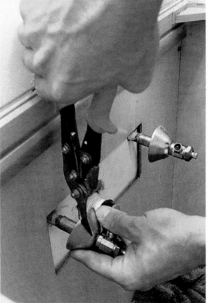

Prep the pipes. Escutcheons will interfere with the old cabinet removal and new cabinet installation, so remove them with metal-cutting snips.

The top goes first. Use a stiff prybar to separate the countertop from the cabinet, and lift the whole top, complete with faucet, from the old vanity.

Screws are last. Back out the screws holding the cabinet to the wall studs, being careful not to strip their heads.

Up then out. When removing the cabinet, lift up and away from the wall, being careful not to bend plumbing stub outs.

starting the demolition, unpack the new vanity and inspect it for defects or damage, and double-check measurements to be sure that the location of the existing plumbing will be compatible with the placement and size of the new cabinet. You don't want to discover that you chose the wrong replacement vanity after the old one is already sitting at the curb for trash pickup.

Fit the cabinet

Scribing—a transferring technique used to cut the cabinet for a perfect fit against the walls and floor—elevates the quality of your vanity installation and eliminates the need to caulk and to hide irregularities created by shimming. For vanity cabinets that have a solid back, this process needs to be done in two phases: an initial scribe to level the cabinet and fit it against the side wall, and then, after the back has been cut so that it can be slid into position against the back wall, a second round of scribing for a final fit (p. 213). The process isn't hard to learn, but the sequencing has to be correct.

Use a level to span the gap. Slide the cabinet as close to final position as the plumbing stub outs will allow, then set a level across the cabinet to mark where its top edge will contact the rear wall.

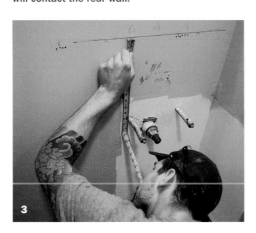

Establish a reference line. Pull the cabinet out of the way, and then extend the level line across the wall from that point.

Measure and record. Measure each pipe position relative to two points—the corner of the wall and the horizontal reference line—then mark the measurements on the wall.

Transfer to the cabinet back. Using the cabinet's side and top edges as your reference points, mark the location where each pipe will protrude through the cabinet back.

Holes in two steps. Drill penetrations using a hole saw slightly larger than the diameter of the pipes. Start from the back side, stopping when the pilot bit pokes through, then use that hole to position the drill bit to finish the hole from the inside.

Scribe the back edge. The drilled holes allow the cabinet to slide into final position against the back wall, where it can be shimmed level and then scribed along the back edge of the side panel so it fits tight to the wall.

Final scribing. With the cabinet in place, do a fine-scribe along the side where it meets the floor and wall, and scribe the bottom and right end of the applied toe kick before cutting the excess from the left end and installing.

Shim the gap. Fasten the cabinet to the rear wall with screws long enough to penetrate at least 1½ in. into the studs, being sure to drive them through the fastening rail near the top edge. When fastening to the side wall, add scraps of wood and/or shims to match the width of the scribed filler strip.

How Much Filler Do I Need?

The vanity will come with a filler strip that is wider than necessary, allowing you to rip it to whatever width you need. That width is determined by the countertop overhang and by how far from flat and plumb your wall is. If the wall is relatively plumb, attach the filler strip and then rip it to leave an extra ⅛ in. for doing the final scribe later.

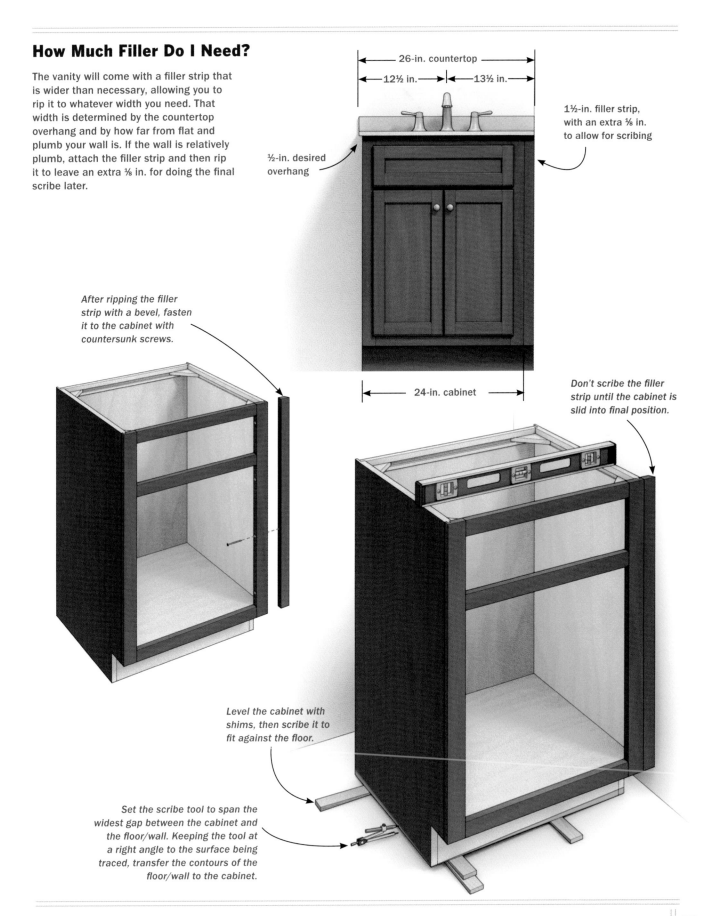

26-in. countertop

12½ in.

13½ in.

1½-in. filler strip, with an extra ⅛ in. to allow for scribing

½-in. desired overhang

24-in. cabinet

After ripping the filler strip with a bevel, fasten it to the cabinet with countersunk screws.

Don't scribe the filler strip until the cabinet is slid into final position.

Level the cabinet with shims, then scribe it to fit against the floor.

Set the scribe tool to span the widest gap between the cabinet and the floor/wall. Keeping the tool at a right angle to the surface being traced, transfer the contours of the floor/wall to the cabinet.

Get a good mark. A strip of painter's tape makes a pencil-friendly path for marking hard, glossy countertops with a scribe tool.

Sand to fit. Solid-surface counters can be cut and shaped with carbide tools and then sanded down to a scribe line using an angle grinder equipped with a sanding disk.

Easy access. It's much easier to install and align the faucet before setting the countertop than it is to reach underneath after it's installed.

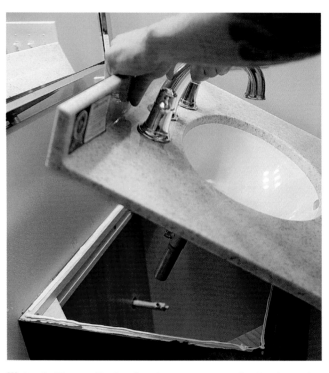

Wet set. After confirming that the countertop scribe fits the wall, apply adhesive caulk to the inside edge of the cabinet to avoid visible squeeze out as the top is set and taped into place to cure.

Countertop and plumbing come last

Install as much of the faucet plumbing as you can prior to setting the countertop. This not only reduces the gymnastics of working in a dark, cramped vanity cabinet, but it makes it easy to ensure that the handles and spout are aligned correctly and spaced evenly. When installing the drain assembly, don't reuse parts from the old vanity. The cost savings would be minimal, but even if drain parts were expensive, it still would not be worth the potential for leaks. On that note, you can leave the cabinet empty for a few days just to make sure there are no leaks. It's easier to adjust a drain trap or snug up a compression fitting than to replace an entire vanity because of an unnoticed leak.

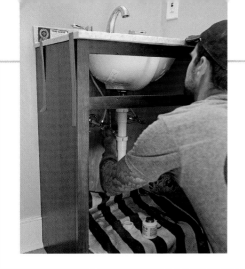

Undersink success

Most faucet packages include all of the components you see from the finished side of the sink, and sometimes even supply lines. The rest of the drain assembly and optional escutcheons must be purchased separately. It pays to spend the time planning what you need up front; otherwise, you'll spend it making multiple drives to the home center or plumbing store for the parts you forgot.

Sink Plumbing

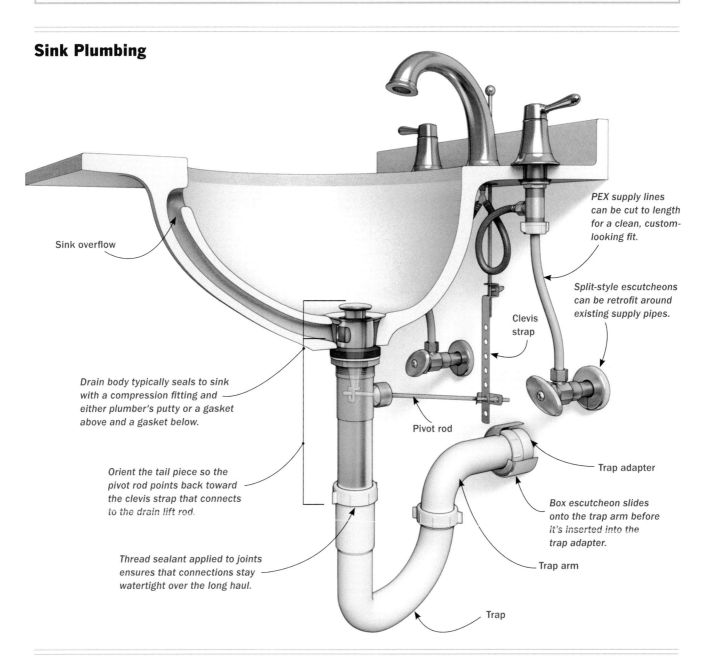

Sink overflow

PEX supply lines can be cut to length for a clean, custom-looking fit.

Split-style escutcheons can be retrofit around existing supply pipes.

Clevis strap

Drain body typically seals to sink with a compression fitting and either plumber's putty or a gasket above and a gasket below.

Pivot rod

Trap adapter

Orient the tail piece so the pivot rod points back toward the clevis strap that connects to the drain lift rod.

Box escutcheon slides onto the trap arm before it's inserted into the trap adapter.

Thread sealant applied to joints ensures that connections stay watertight over the long haul.

Trap arm

Trap

Contributors

Longtime *Fine Woodworking* contributing editor **Christian Becksvoort** is a professional furniture maker in Maine and a well-known expert on Shaker furniture design.

Brent Benner owns The Roxbury Cabinet Company in Roxbury, Conn.

Aaron Butt is a lead carpenter with Carpenter & MacNeille Architects and Builders in Essex, Mass.

Michael Cullen makes furniture in Petaluma, Calif.

Marianne Cusato is the author of *Get Your House Right: Architectural Elements to Use and Avoid.*

Paul DeGroot is an architect in Austin, Texas (degrootarchitect.com), and a regular contributor to *Fine Homebuilding.*

Rodney Diaz is *Fine Homebuilding's* creative director.

A former fighter pilot and retired software engineer, **Steve Fikar** lives in Shalimar, Fla.

Justin Fink is the former editorial director of *Fine Homebuilding.*

Tyler Grace is a *Fine Homebuilding* ambassador and the owner of TRG Home Concepts in Haddon Heights, N.J.

Larissa Huff and **Rob Spiece** run Lohr School of Woodworking in Schwenksville, Pa., and make custom furniture.

Mark Hutker, FAIA, has been practicing architecture for over 30 years. He owns Hutker Architects on Cape Cod in Massachusetts.

Paul Johnson runs Paul Johnson Carpentry and Remodeling in Portland, Ore.

Clark Kellogg is a professional furniture maker in Houston, Texas.

Mike Korsak makes custom furniture in Pittsburgh, Pa.

Fine Woodworking contributing editor **Steve Latta** teaches woodworking at Thaddeus Stevens College in Lancaster, Pa.

Matthew Millham is a former deputy editor of *Fine Homebuilding.*

Philip Morley builds furniture in Wimberley, Texas.

Michael Pekovich is a furniture maker, woodworking teacher, and *Fine Woodworking's* editor and creative director. He is the author of *Foundations of Woodworking* from The Taunton Press.

Nathan Rinne is a finish carpenter in Roach, Mo.

Mario Rodriguez makes furniture and teaches woodworking in Philadelphia.

Willie Sandry is a woodworker and small-scale lumber kiln operator in Camas, Wash.

Stefan Straka owns North Cascade Creative, a professional cabinet and furniture shop in Bellingham, Wash.

Gary Striegler is a trim carpenter in Fayetteville, Ark.

Suzanne Walton is the owner of Rowan Woodwork in Kingston, N.Y., where Owen Madden is lead builder.

Credits

All photos are courtesy of *Fine Homebuilding magazine (FHB)*, © The Taunton Press, Inc., or *Fine Woodworking (FWW)* magazine, © The Taunton Press, Inc., except as noted below:

Front cover: left photo by Mike Korsak, right top photo by Jody Lawson, right bottom photo by Brian Vanden Brink. Back cover drawing by John Hartman.

The articles in this book appeared in the following issues of *Fine Homebuilding* and *Fine Woodworking*:

pp. 4–9: Guide to Sheet Goods by Suzanne Walton and Owen Madden, FWW issue 295. Photos by Michael Pekovich except photo p. 4 and bottom right photo p. 6 by Jane Messinger, bottom photos p. 5 and bottom right photo p. 9 by Chris Kendall, bottom left photo p. 6 by Ofer Wolberger, bottom left photo p. 7 by Nils Schlebusch, bottom right photo p. 7 and bottom left photo p. 9 by Suzanne Walton, bottom left photo p. 8 by Kyle J. Caldwell, and bottom right photo p. 8 by Anissa Kapsales.

pp. 10–15: All You Need Is a Track Saw by Justin Fink, FHB issue 276. Photos by Rodney Diaz. Drawings by Trevor Johnston.

pp. 16–21: Lightweight Crosscut Sled for Large Panels by Steve Fikar, FWW issue 292. Photos by Asa Christiana. Drawings by Vince Babak.

pp. 22–29: Anchor Your Work to the Wall by Mario Rodriguez, FWW issues 291. Action photos by Jonathan Binzen and fastener photos by Michael Pekovich.

pp. 30–39: Elegant Bookcase Top to Bottom by Mike Korsak, FWW issue 264. Photos by Jonathan Binzen except photos p. 30 and p. 32 by Mike Korsak. Drawings by John Hartman.

pp. 40–50: Arts-and-Crafts Bookcase by Willie Sandry, FWW issue 274. Photos by FWW staff. Drawings by John Hartman.

pp. 51–61: Build a Night Stand by Michael Cullen, FWW issue 247. Photos by Jonathan Binzen except photo p. 51 by Don Russel. Drawings by Kelly J. Dunton.

pp. 62–69: Ship-Inspired Wall Shelf by Christian Becksvoort, FWW issue 288. Photos by Anissa Kapsales. Drawings by Dan Thornton.

pp. 70–79: Modern Wall Shelf by Christian Becksvoort, FWW issue 284. Photos by Anissa Kapsales except photo p. 70 and bottom left photo p. 79 by Michael Pekovich. Drawings by John Hartman.

pp. 80–92: A Bevy of Built-Ins by Rodney Diaz, FHB issue 303. Photos by Jody Lawson. Drawings by Christopher Mills.

pp. 93–99: Built-Ins for Odd Spaces by Gary Striegler, FHB issue 298. Photos by Matthew Millham.

pp. 100–107: Build a Desk Bed by Nathan Rinnie, FHB issue 283. Photos by Patrick Mc-Combe except photo p. 100 by David Dilks, courtesy of Nathan Rinne. Drawings by Christopher Mills.

pp. 108–111: Spaces within Spaces by Mark Hutker, FHB issue 257. Photos p. 109 and bottom photo p. 110 by Brian Vanden Brink. Top photo p. 110 and photos p. 111 by Eric Roth. Floor-plan drawings by Martha Garstang Hill.

pp. 112–116: Custom Cabinets: An Inside Look by Brent Benner, FHB issue 271. Photos by Brian Vanden Brink except photo p. 115 by Charles Miller. Drawings by Christopher Mills.

pp. 117–129: Installing Frameless Cabinets by Aaron Butt, FHB issue 293. Photos by Patrick McCombe.

pp. 130–140: Contemporary Wall Cabinet by Philip Morley, FWW issue 292. Photos by Jonathan Binzen. Drawings by Christopher Mills.

pp. 141–151: Wall Cabinet with Curves by Clark Kellogg, FWW issue 263. Photos by Matt Kenney. Drawings by Christopher Mills.

pp. 152–159: Building with Rabbets and Dadoes by Michael Pekovich, FWW issue 290. Photos by Rachel Barclay except photo p. 152 by Michael Pekovich. Drawings by John Hartman.

pp. 160–171: A Better-Built Cabinet by Steve Latta, FWW issue 284. Photos by Barry NM Dima except left photo p. 160 by Michael Pekovich. Drawings by Christopher Mills.

pp. 172–178: Use Vintage Glass for Cabinet Doors by Steve Latta, FWW issue 256. Photos by Jonathan Binzen except photo p. 172 and left photos p. 173 by Michael Pekovich.

pp. 179–185: Foolproof Inset Cabinet Doors by Stefan Straka, FHB issue 304. Photos by Asa Christiana.

pp. 186–193: Contemporary Door and Drawer Pull by Larissa Huff and Robert Spiece, FWW issue 289. Photos by Anissa Kapsales. Drawings by Dan Thornton.

pp. 194–195: Build a Custom Rollout Cabinet by Paul Johnson, FHB issue 270. Photos by Nina Johnson. Drawings by Christopher Mills.

pp. 196–201: Practical Makes Perfect by Matthew Millham, FHB issue 279. Photo p. 196 by Rob Karosis and photo p. 201 by Mark Luthringer. Drawings by Christopher Mills.

pp. 202–205: Drawing Board: Multipurpose kitchen islands by Paul DeGroot, FHB issue 263. Drawings by Paul DeGroot.

pp. 206–208: Design Build: Bathroom Vanities by Marianne Cusato, FHB issue 271. Photo courtesy of Eviva (eviva.us). Drawings by Marianne Cusato.

pp. 209–215: Replace Your Vanity by Tyler Grace, FHB issue 263. Photos by Aaron Fagan. Drawings by Christopher Mills.

Index